D1168735

MEDITATION
AND ITS
PRACTICE

MEDITATION
AND ITS
PRACTICE

Swami Rama

The Himalayan International Institute
of Yoga Science and Philosophy
of the U.S.A.
Honesdale, Pennsylvania

© 1992 by Swami Rama

*Himalayan International Institute
of Yoga Science and Philosophy of the U.S.A.
RR 1, Box 400
Honesdale, Pennsylvania 18431*

05 04 03 02 01 00 99 98 97 96   6 5 4 3 2

All rights reserved. No part of this book may be reproduced in any form or by any means without permission in writing from the publisher. Printed in the United States of America.

♾ *The paper used in this publication meets the minimum requirements of the American National Standard for Information Sciences—Permanence of Paper for Printed Library Materials, ANSI Z39.48-1984.*

Library of Congress Cataloging-in-Publication Data

Rama, Swami, 1925–
    Meditation and its practice/by Swami Rama.
       p. cm.
    ISBN 0-89389-130-4
    1. Meditation. I. Title.
BL627.R3365 1991
158'.12—dc20

Contents

Foreword

I n the past twenty years, meditation has integrated itself into modern life and become an increasingly familiar word in our vocabulary. Physicians, psychologists, and other professionals endorse meditation as a powerful tool for relieving stress, maintaining health, and promoting creativity and vitality. These developments have been facilitated by the work of Swami Rama, who has had a unique impact on our scientific understanding of the mind and body through his participation in research on meditation and meditative states.

As Swami Rama makes clear in this concise and practical text, meditation is a powerful technique that anyone can use to increase physiological balance, clarity of mind, and awareness of the subtlest levels of our being. Even those who have not yet achieved deep states of meditation can learn to create stillness of body and mind and will notice many benefits of this stillness.

This volume presents meditation in a clear and precise language that is free of religion or cultural influences, so that the practice of meditation can be easily understood and accepted by the modern reader. I am sure that many will be grateful for this lucid and inspiring introduction to the practice of meditation.

Kay Gendron, Ph.D.

Acknowledgments

The author would like to thank Kamal Hafford and Darlene Clark, who typeset this book, as well as Anil Saklani for book design. Dave Gorman and Wendy Hoffman served as photographic subjects for Lyle Olson. Kay Gendron, Ph.D., edited this book and helped prepare the manuscript. Dr. John Clarke, M.D., kindly reviewed the book.

Preface

This book was written to provide a clear, systematic manual of the basic techniques of meditation and the most important practices used in preparing to meditate. It is meant to give you a progressive, step-by-step approach that is practical rather than merely philosophical or theoretical.

For thousands of years, the science of meditation has been practiced and studied by aspirants who sought to make their lives more serene, creative, and fulfilling. Meditation will give you the capacity to improve your health, your relationships, and the skillfulness of all of your activities. This is because meditation can do something that no other technique can accomplish—it introduces you to yourself on all levels, and finally leads you to the center of consciousness within, from where consciousness flows on various degrees and levels. This center of consciousness is called *Atman*. The seeker's aspirations are fulfilled when he or she becomes fully aware of Atman, the inner dweller, and then no longer identifies with the objects of the mind and the world.

When this occurs, the aspirant becomes established in the realm of Atman, and that is also termed *samadhi*. After attaining this state, all problems are resolved and all questions are answered.

While the basic practices are very simple to learn, you

will find that the more consistently and regularly you practice, the more you will know the benefits. At first, you may notice simple changes, such as increased calmness and resistance to stress, but as you progress you will notice deeper and more significant developments within yourself. This inward journey is very pleasant, provided you are persistent and practice regularly.

In fact, the practical science of meditation is so profound and interesting that you may find yourself intrigued and challenged by other aspects of yoga, including *asanas* (physical yoga postures), the science of breath, issues related to improving your health, and the underlying psychology or philosophy of meditation. May you enjoy and benefit from the process you have begun.

1

What Is Meditation?

Meditation is a word that has been used in a variety of ways, and thus, there is a good deal of confusion about what precisely meditation is and how it is practiced. Some people mistakenly use the word "meditate" to mean thinking or contemplating; others use it to refer to a state such as daydreaming or fantasizing. However, meditation is not any of these mere experiences; it is a distinct and different process, which is important to fully understand.

Meditation is a specific technique for completely resting the mind and attaining a state of consciousness that is totally different than the normal waking state. In meditation, you are fully awake and alert, but the mind is not focused on the external world or the events taking place around you. Neither is the mind asleep, dreaming, or fantasizing. Instead, the mind is clear, relaxed, and focused "within."

The root of the word "meditation" is similar to the root word for "medical" or "medicate," and the root of all these words implies the sense of "attending to" or "paying attention to" something. In meditation, you pay attention to dimensions of yourself that are seldom observed or known—that is, your own deepest, inner levels. These deeper levels are more profound than the processes of thinking, analyzing, day-dreaming, or experiencing emotions or memories. Meditation involves a type of "inner attention" that is quiet, concentrated, and at the same time, relaxed. There is nothing strenuous or difficult about creating this "inner attention"; in fact, you will find that meditation is a process that is restful and relaxing for the mind. In the beginning, the greatest difficulty is that the mind has never been trained in how to create this inner attention.

In every culture and society, all over the world, people are educated in the skills needed to function and survive in that culture—how to talk, think, work, and investigate the objects and experiences of the external world. We learn sciences such as biology, ecology, and chemistry in order to understand the world we live in, but no one teaches us to understand or attend to our own inner dimensions, not in any school, college or university. We merely learn to assimilate the goals, fashions, and values of our society, without really knowing ourselves first, within and without. This leaves us ignorant of ourselves and dependent on the advice and suggestions of others.

Meditation is a very different, subtle, and precise approach; it is a simple technique of learning to pay attention to and understand all the various levels of ourselves—the body, the breathing process, the aspects of stress. As time progresses, you may find that you enjoy the positive results of meditation—increased joyfulness, clarity, and awareness—as much as you enjoy the relief of the physical, nervous, and mental symptoms of stress.

This meditation manual systematically offers guidance in the practice of meditation and will answer the most common questions about getting started. With these techniques you can continue on your own for some time. Ultimately, there are stages in meditation where external guidance from an experienced meditator is beneficial and necessary. However, this manual will help you with the most important, basic practices. You will find that you do not need to do anything physically different or demanding, that your meditation does not require you to adopt any strange or foreign habits, and that you do not have to be able to meditate for long or extended periods of time in order to progress and observe the benefits. You will enjoy the practice of meditation! Your body will be more relaxed, your mind will become more creative and focused, and you may even notice significant improvements in your health and relationships!

Meditation is therapeutic from the very beginning; it helps relax the tension of the gross and subtle muscles and the autonomic nervous system, and it provides freedom from mental stress. A person of meditation attains a tranquil mind, and this helps the immune system by limiting its reaction to stress and strain. You will find that even a few days' sincere efforts will help you to control your appetites and even reactions such as anger to a certain degree. Meditation will also decrease the need for sleep and energize the body and mind. This is a result we have observed with students from all walks of life.

Those who are writers, poets, and thinkers often express interest in the process of becoming creative and using their intuition, the finest and most evolved of all aspects of knowledge. Meditation is a systematic way of using this aspect of human brilliance in our daily life.

Meditation also has an important influence on health. In the modern world, most diseases can be classified to some degree as psychosomatic, having their origins in or being influenced by the human mind, thoughts, and emotions. Recently, scientists have begun to recognize that these kinds of diseases cannot really be "cured" merely by the conventional methods of orthodox medicine or psychotherapy alone, because if disease originates in the mind and emotional reactions, how can an external therapy alone restore your health? If you rely only on external remedies, and do not seek to understand your own mind and emotions, you may merely become dependent on a therapist or physician for help. In contrast, the method of meditation makes people self-reliant and helps them to attain the inner strength necessary to deal more effectively with all life's problems.

Meditation as a Process

In the process of meditation, we ask the mind to let go of its tendencies to think, analyze, remember, solve problems, and focus on the events of the past or on the expectations of the future. We help the mind to slow down its rapid series of thoughts and feelings, and to replace that mental activity with an inner awareness and attention. Thus, meditation is not *thinking about* problems or analyzing a situation. It is not fantasizing or daydreaming or merely letting the mind wander aimlessly. Meditation is not having an internal conversation or argument with yourself or intensifying the thinking process. Meditation is simply a quiet, effortless, one-pointed focus of attention and awareness.

In meditation, we try to let go of all the many mental distractions, preoccupations, and the fleeting thoughts and associations of our normal waking experience. We do this, not by trying to make the mind empty, which is impossible, but instead, by allowing the mind to focus on one subtle element or object, which leads the attention further inward. By giving the mind one internal focus of attention, we help the mind to cease its other stressful mental processes, such as worry, planning, thinking, and reasoning.

In our tradition, the student of meditation may be given an internal device or "object" to help concentrate the mind. Most often, a sound is used in this manner, although sometimes a visual image for concentration is suggested. These may be either gross (external) or subtle, according to the frame of mind of the aspirant. Sounds which are used to concentrate the mind in meditation are called *mantras*, and they have very powerful effects on the mental level.

A mantra may be a word, a phrase, a set of sounds or simply a syllable. Concentrating on a mantra helps the student to let go of other useless, distracting mental processes, and allows one to go deeper. Many different kinds of mantras are used throughout the world, including mantras such as *Om*, *Amen*, and *Shalom*, and all have the goal of helping to focus the mind. In this manual, we will introduce a basic mantra for your practice. Using that mantra regularly will be most beneficial.

In all the great spiritual traditions of the world, ancient and modern, there is some system of pronouncing such a syllable, sound or set of words that acts like a mantra. This is a profound and great science, and those who are competent in this science can lead students on the path. The preliminaries practiced by aspirants are simple and easy, but when one begins to deal with the mind, the prescription of an appropriate mantra can be seen to be very effective and powerful.

The meditative texts and scriptures speak extensively on this subject. Patanjali, the codifier of the yoga science, says that the mantra becomes a representative of the innermost source of consciousness. Therefore, it becomes a leader and even a bridge between the mortal and immortal parts of life. When the body, breath, and conscious mind separate from the unconscious mind and the individual soul, the conscious effort of having remembered such a mantra goes on creating impressions in the unconscious. These impressions are powerful motivations, which help the aspirant during the period of transition we call death, and then it becomes easier for him or her to make the unknown voyage.

Mantra is a support and is the focal point given to the mind. Teachers make the choice of prescribing a mantra according to the state of mind of the aspirant and the burning desire he or she holds within.

Just as there are many different paths one could take to climb a mountain, there are a variety of seemingly "different" meditation practices or techniques. Yet all have the same goal—achieving a state of inner concentration, calmness, and serenity. Any practice that helps you to achieve this is beneficial. Many valid techniques exist, so there is really no difference between one type of authentic meditation and another, as long as they have the goal of helping you to attain this inner stillness and focus.

Sometimes, people become very caught up in comparing meditation techniques or arguing about which tradition or teacher is "best." Good meditation teachers recognize and respect the universal aspect of meditation and do not foster petty, self-serving or cultish distinctions about "their" techniques. Meditation is a very beneficial and fruitful way of exploring the inner dimensions and fathoming all the levels of life systematically. It is positive and valuable, as long as teachers do not become egotistical and try to claim a "brand" of meditation as their own or compare their techniques with other varieties of meditation.

In the beginning, the aspirant does not have the clarity of mind needed to understand or discover the correct method of meditation, and may be easily caught up or influenced by teachers who promote their own type of meditation. Sadly, some of these teachers are dishonest and do not even really practice meditation themselves. Many students waste valuable time and energy seeking an authentic meditative discipline, jumping from one path to another. After spending much time, energy, and money on this quest they may become frustrated and disappointed and then stop making a sincere effort.

In the Himalayan tradition, we sometimes say that if there is any such thing as "sin" in the world, it is confusing or misleading sincere students. This is not to imply that the method of meditation we teach is right and that others are wrong, but simply to say that meditation is not a religious ritual or a part of any religion, but a pure and simple method of exploring the inner dimensions of life and finally establishing oneself in one's own essential nature. Some schools call it *samadhi*, others *nirvana*; some call it *perfection* or *enlightenment*. It can also be called *Christ-consciousness*. Such words and labels do not matter at all. The system of meditation teaches inner spirituality, not any particular religion.

If we observe life clearly, we realize that from our childhood onward, we have only been trained and educated in how to examine and verify things in the external world and that no one has actually taught us how to look within, find within, and verify within. Therefore, the human being remains a stranger to himself or herself, while trying to establish various sorts of relationships in the external world. That is why none of these relationships really seems to work successfully, and confusion and disappointment prevail.

Very little of the mind is cultivated by our formal educational system. The part of the mind that dreams and sleeps, the vast realm of the unconscious, which is the reservoir of all our experiences, remains unknown and undisciplined; it is not subject to any control. It is true that "the whole of the body is in the mind, but the whole of the mind is not in the body." There is no other method to truly develop control over the totality of the mind except through the practice of meditation.

We are taught how to move and behave in the external world, but we are never taught how to be still and examine what is within ourselves. At the same time, learning to be still and calm should not be made a ceremony or a part of any religion; it is a universal requirement of the human body. When one learns to sit still, he or she attains a kind of joy that is inexplicable. The highest of all joys that can ever be attained or experienced by a human being can be attained through meditation. All the other joys in the world are transient and momentary, but the joy of meditation is immense and everlasting. This is not being extreme or exaggerating, but simply stating a truth that is supported by the long line of the great sages, both those who renounced the world and attained Truth, and also those who lived in the world and yet renounced, unaffected.

The mind has a tendency to wander into the "grooves"

of its old habit patterns, and then it imagines those experiences in the future. The mind does not really know how to be in the present, here and now. Only meditation teaches us to fully experience the now, which is part of the eternal. When, with the help of meditative techniques, the mind is made one-pointed and inward, it attains the power of penetrating into the deeper levels of one's being. Then, the mind does not create any distractions or deviations; it fully attains the power of concentration, which is a prerequisite for meditation.

How fortunate are those who become aware of this fact and begin to meditate! Even more fortunate are those who continue to meditate, and the fortunate few are those who have decided and determined that meditation is the priority of their life, and thus practice it regularly.

To begin this path, understand clearly what meditation is, select a practice that is comfortable for you, and do it consistently and regularly for some time, every day if possible, and at the same time every day. In the modern world, however, students tend to become impatient easily and to do a practice for only a brief period of time before they give up, concluding that there is no value or authenticity to the technique. This is like a child who plants a tulip bulb and is frustrated because he sees no flowers in a week! You will definitely experience progress if you meditate regularly—it is not possible for you to fail to progress if you do the practice.

At first, you may see the progress in terms of immediate physical relaxation and calmness. Later, you may notice other, more subtle, benefits. Some of the most important benefits of meditation make themselves known gradually over time, and are not dramatic or easily observed. Persist in your meditation and you will experience progress. Later, we will discuss how to observe and assess your progress and when to move on to the next step.

Before we conclude this discussion, we will try to clarify the distinctions between some concepts that are often confused with meditation.

Meditation Is not Contemplation or Thinking

Contemplation, especially the contemplation of inspiring concepts or ideals—such as truth, peace, and love—can be very helpful, although it is distinct and different than the process of meditation. In contemplation, you engage your mind in inquiry into this concept, and ask it to consider the meaning and value of the concept. In the system of meditation, contemplation is considered a separate practice, although one that also may be very useful at some times. When you engage in meditation, you do not ask the mind to think about or contemplate on any concept, but rather, to go beyond this level of mental activity.

Meditation Is not Hypnosis or Autosuggestion

In hypnosis, a suggestion is made to the mind, either by another person or yourself. Such a suggestion may take the form, "You are getting sleepy (or relaxed)." Thus, in hypnosis, there is an attempt to program, manipulate or control the content of the mind, to make it believe a certain fact or think in an ordered, particular way. Sometimes, such suggestions can have useful effects, as suggestion is very powerful. Unfortunately, negative suggestions very commonly have negative effects on us or our health.

In meditation, you do not make any attempt to give the mind a direct suggestion or to control the mind. You simply observe and let the mind become quiet and calm, allowing your mantra to lead you deeper within, exploring and experiencing the deeper levels of your being. In the meditative traditions, a practice such as hypnosis is thought to have some potential liabilities—it may create conflict or resistance in the mind because of the force or external influence used in the suggestion. Practices such as hypnosis or autosuggestion may have some therapeutic place, but it is important not to confuse them with meditation. The sages say that meditation is actually the opposite of hypnosis—a state of clarity and freedom from suggestion or influence.

Meditation Is not Religion

Meditation is not some strange or foreign practice that requires you to change your beliefs, your culture or your religion. Meditation is not a religion at all, but rather a very practical, scientific, and systematic technique for knowing yourself on all levels. Meditation does not "belong to" any culture or religion of the world. Some misguided people promote practices they call meditation, but which are really a mingling of pure meditation with religion or cultural influences and values. This causes others to become confused or anxious that meditation will interfere with their religion or beliefs, or that they will have to give up their own culture and take on another culture's practice. This is not the case: Religion teaches people what to believe, but meditation teaches you to experience directly for yourself. There is no conflict between these two techniques. Worship is a part of the religious system, as is prayer, which is a dialogue with the divine principle. Certainly, you can be both a religious person who prays and also be a meditator who uses the techniques of meditation, but it is not necessary to have an orthodox religion to meditate. Meditation should be practiced as a pure technique, in a systematic, orderly way.

In order to meditate, you will need to learn:

　　1) How to relax the body;

　　2) How to sit in a comfortable, steady position for meditation;

　　3) How to make your breathing process serene;

　　4) How to witness the objects traveling in the train of the mind;

　　5) How to inspect the quality of thoughts and learn to promote or strengthen those which are positive and helpful in your growth;

6) How not to allow yourself to become disturbed in any situation, whether you judge it to
be either bad or good.

This book will systematically cover all these aspects,
so that your meditation becomes enjoyable, deep, and
effective. If you practice meditation with a clear understanding of what it is, and with the appropriate technique
and attitudes, you will find it refreshing and energizing.
Now that you understand these basic issues, you are ready
for the next step—preparing to meditate!

2

Preparation for Meditation

T he most important and most often overlooked step in meditation is that of preparation. Without the appropriate preparation, physical, mental or emotional distractions will create obstacles that prevent your meditation from being deep or profound. And while the physical body does not itself produce the meditative state or help you meditate, physical problems or discomforts can certainly create barriers or distractions in your meditation.

The most common physical barriers are:

(a) illness;

(b) physical discomfort caused by tension or an inability to relax so that you can sit comfortably;

(c) fatigue or drowsiness;

(d) being physically agitated, jittery or restless from the day's stressful events;

(e) problems with food: either being hungry or having eaten excessively.

Most of the common physical barriers to meditation can be eliminated by becoming increasingly aware of how you manage your lifestyle. Of course, it's true that prevention is better than cure. While you can certainly continue to meditate with a cold or a minor physical problem, you will probably find that the discomfort, pain or inability to concentrate that accompanies any severe illness is a real barrier to meditation. Fortunately, meditation tends to make you more sensitive to many physical processes, helping you to prevent illness by becoming more attuned to what your body needs in order to stay well.

Recommendations for how to remove these barriers will all be given in this manual. Special attention and practices will be provided for the removal of physical tension and stress. In addition, the issues of food and adequate sleep, and how they affect meditation practice, will be described later in this chapter.

Creating a Time and Place for Meditation

An advanced meditator can sit in meditation almost anywhere. For most of us, however, paying attention to some basic guidelines will greatly increase the ease of meditation. No special or unusual prerequisites for meditation exist—you can meditate at home, in the country, in the city, at the shore or in the mountains. It does help, however, if the general environment is good and the place you have chosen for meditation is relatively quiet, peaceful, uncluttered, and restful.

Ideally, a small corner of your room or home can be set aside as your meditation space. This should have good air circulation and not be stuffy, musty or uncomfortable. A clean, quiet place is all you need. It is best if this space is apart from the main "busy-ness" of your life—away from the kitchen, television or telephone—and not where others will interrupt you. Similarly, it may be wise to avoid a place like an office, which may have associations that distract you mentally. Choose a quiet, pleasant corner or area of a room. It is not recommended that you meditate on your bed because your mental associations with sleep may make it hard to stay alert and awake there. Whether you sit on a chair or on the floor as described in the next chapter, it helps to select a special place and reserve it for meditation.

Finding Time to Meditate

Meditation can be done at any time of night or day, but traditionally, the "best" times, when the circumstances are most conducive to meditation, are early mornings or late evenings, when the environment begins to "quiet down" and you are not likely to be interrupted by others. If you are a parent with small children, it will probably be easiest to meditate when the children are in bed. At first, try to select one or two brief periods (5-15 minutes) when you can meditate without inconveniencing others, being disturbed, ignoring your duties or feeling rushed or preoccupied by other tasks. If you rise a little earlier in the morning or meditate just prior to bed at night, you may find it easiest to adjust your routine.

Some people seem to be "naturally" freshest and more alert in the morning or the evening. That may be your own best time to meditate. However, your schedule and your personal responsibilities may also have a great impact on when you meditate.

Maintain a Regular Time

You will find that your meditation progresses most rapidly if you create a regular time that you can reserve for meditation every day. Establishing this mental habit and making it a reliable, predictable part of your schedule are extremely beneficial in deepening practice. Even if your schedule shifts from day to day, try to find a time and be consistent and regular at that time, as much as possible. This helps to eliminate the mental resistance caused by laziness and the tendency to procrastinate.

First Step: Preparing for a Meditation Session

First, prepare the body physically. Meditation is easiest when the body feels fresh, comfortable, relaxed, and clean. Taking a shower or even simply washing your face, hands, and feet will help to give you a fresher feeling.

In the morning, your body will feel most comfortable meditating if you empty your bladder and bowels after you rise and then prepare for meditation.

Second Step: Relax and Stretch the Muscles

Some people find that their bodies feel stiff and achy after sleeping all night. In such cases, a warm bath and gentle stretching exercises may help to prepare your body to sit in meditation.

The hatha yoga asanas (postures) were specifically developed to maintain physical health and to help the body sit comfortably in meditation. They make the body supple. While a detailed lesson in hatha yoga is not possible in this book, some basic postures that are beneficial in preparing for meditation are taught in *Hatha Yoga Manual I* and *II*. (Ideally, asanas should be learned personally from a qualified instructor.)

Stretching and limbering the back and legs can significantly increase your comfort in meditation. Even a few minutes of stretching exercise or yogic asanas can create a vast improvement in the quality of your meditative experience. Unlike strenuous aerobic exercise, these yoga postures will not fatigue you or create too much activation. Instead, the yoga postures will gently energize you, relax your muscles, help you let go of mental stress, and focus your concentration. In the beginning, consider trying to spend at least 5-10 minutes stretching and preparing the body.

Third Step: Relaxation Practices to Prepare for Meditation

After you complete your stretching exercises you may find it beneficial to do a brief relaxation practice. Lie comfortably, with your back flat on the floor or a padded surface. Lie with your arms down at the sides, palms up. Let your legs be slightly separate, a comfortable distance apart. Make sure that your body weight is evenly distributed and that you are not twisted or leaning to either side. Your head should also be centered, and not tilted in either direction, as this will create tension in the neck. This relaxation position is called the "corpse posture," because in it, you lie very still and relaxed. Let your eyes be gently closed and take several minutes to become aware of your breathing, exhaling and inhaling through the nostrils slowly and smoothly, without any interruptions or pauses.

Lying in this posture, you can lead yourself through a brief relaxation exercise, systematically paying attention to each major muscle group, moving progressively through the body. A complete description of this practice is given in the appendix. You may also be interested in using a guided relaxation tape, available from the Himalayan Publishers. Relaxation practices should be brief, and should not last longer than about 10 minutes. You will need to ask your mind to remain alert and not go to sleep, because for many people, the tendency for the mind to drift off to sleep will become evident.

Fourth Step: Calming the Mind and Nervous System with Breathing Practices

The breathing process is a very powerful variable, which has an enormous impact on the tension level of the body, as well as on the calmness and clarity of the mind. Before meditation, special yogic breathing practices are done in a meditative sitting posture, in order to help create a calm mental state conducive to an inward focus, concentration, and serenity. Some students may initially feel a little resistant to spending a small amount of time on these practices. However, once you have done them, you will probably notice that they aid immeasurably in helping to deepen meditation. The breathing process and its role in emotional balance and mental clarity are fascinating, and later, we will provide several specific breathing exercises that have a vital and beneficial impact on meditation.

Fifth Step: Sitting in Meditation

After you complete your breathing practice, you are ready to meditate. You sit in your meditative posture (which will be described next) and you simply allow your mind to become aware of your own mantra, or the universal mantra, *So Hum*, a sound that is coordinated with the breathing in a special way. As you exhale, you mentally hear the sound *Hum*; as you inhale, you mentally hear the sound *So*.

Let your breath continue to lengthen and become

smooth. You sit quietly and let your mind focus on the mantra. You continue to sit comfortably in your meditation posture, letting your mind become quiet and centered. You may sit for as long as is comfortable or for whatever time you have available on that occasion. When you are ready to end your meditation, you first bring your mental awareness back to the breathing and then to the body. You make the transition to the state of external awareness by gently opening your eyes to look first at the palms of your own hands, or by covering your eyes with cupped hands before you open your eyes. The issue of what happens with the mind in meditation and how you work with the mind will be discussed in greater detail in the following chapter.

Thus, the order of practice is as follows: first, bathing or preparing; second, stretching exercise or yoga postures; third, relaxation exercise; fourth, breathing practices; and finally, meditation itself.

Before we complete this general discussion, there are other important issues related to preparation for meditation that deserve special attention. These include the way that food affects your meditation.

The Influence of Meals on Meditation Time

Meditative psychology describes the presence of four "primitive fountains," which are four drives that motivate human beings. These four drives are the urges for food, sex, sleep, and self-preservation, and these four urges need to be skillfully managed if our meditation is to progress. Imbalances in these four urges have physical and emotional consequences that may interfere significantly with the ability to concentrate and meditate.

From the meditative perspective, a healthy diet is composed chiefly of fresh, simple food that is neither overcooked, overprocessed, greasy, nor excessively roasted or toasted. These attributes tend to cause digestive problems that interfere with meditation. Fresh, simple natural food that is nutritious and easy to digest will be most beneficial.

The atmosphere in which food is eaten should also be pleasant and joyous. In the modern society, in which husbands, wives, and children are busy away from home all day, they only have the opportunity to come together and discuss the day's events at the dining room table. But this time should not be made unpleasant or negative; the family should have the understanding that no unpleasant discussions should occur at that time. Cheerfulness is traditionally said to be the greatest of all physicians, and those who are aware of that know that while they are eating they should be cheerful and pleasant. A pleasant, cheerful state of mind has a powerful effect on the efficiency of the digestive system and the secretion of the endocrine glands.

Many diseases and physical problems can be prevented once we understand the functioning of our body and its language. When good food is eaten in pleasant circumstances and with a pleasant mood, it helps the body to effectively produce saliva and gastric juices, aiding in the digestion of food. When food is eaten in a depressed mood, or during heated, negative discussions, this affects the digestive system and can create digestive disorders.

All food should be well-chewed. It is best to fully enjoy your food by eating slowly and taking the time to taste it. To promote good digestion, there should also be an adequate amount of liquid in the food. Fresh fruits and salads should also be a part of your diet.

Overeating should be avoided, because of the many problems it causes. After a meal, rinse and clean the mouth and teeth, and then allow the digestive system to "rest" without snacking between meals. Food should always be taken at least four hours before meditation, sex or sleep. Eating food and then immediately retiring to bed is not a healthy habit.

The process of digestion and your body's reaction to foods can have powerful influences on your meditation. In fact, one cannot really meditate for three to four hours after eating a significant meal. For this reason, the early morning hours are ideal for meditation—your body should be finished with digesting the previous day's food and should feel light and fresh. In the evening, you will find that if you eat a late, heavy dinner, you will have to wait until fairly late at night to be able to really concentrate or meditate.

Obviously, the kind of foods you eat will cause a range of different results: A light, fresh meal of easily digested vegetables, fruits, and grains may not take much time to digest, while a very heavy "feast" with rich, fatty foods may take hours. Further, you will probably find yourself increasingly aware that certain foods help you to feel clear, relaxed, and "centered" while you meditate. Conversely, foods may also cause a variety of interferences. Some foods will make you restless, agitated, and tense, creating a jittery feeling. Other foods may make you drowsy, sleepy or sluggish, creating so much heaviness you can barely remain awake in meditation. As you continue to experiment with your reaction to foods you will become increasingly aware of how particular foods affect your own meditation.

It is not necessary that you become a vegetarian in order to meditate. In fact, if you don't know how to create a well-balanced vegetarian diet, an abrupt change in your eating patterns could cause you some significant difficulties. A well-balanced vegetarian diet, with fresh fruits, dairy products, and well-cooked vegetables, grains, and legumes, may be very helpful, particularly if it is low in fat. As you continue your meditation, your attractions to foods (as well as many other things!) may gradually evolve in a healthier direction. If you decide to make changes in your diet, you may want to first consult a resource book such as *Transition to Vegetarianism*[1] to guide your efforts.

The effects of food and beverages on the depth of meditation are very powerful, and as indicated, you may become increasingly skilled in noticing the subtle effects of what you eat or drink. Many people who initially drink large amounts of coffee, tea or other caffeinated

1. *Transition to Vegetarianism* by Rudolph M. Ballentine, M.D. is available from the Himalayan Publishers.

beverages begin to notice how this creates physical and mental agitation. The topic of food and its effect on meditation and consciousness is so powerful and important that it actually deserves an entire book; however, some basic suggestions are:

-Before you meditate, try to allow 3-4 hours after a main meal;
-Be aware of what you have eaten and how it affects your meditation later in the day;
-Select fresh, wholesome, easy-to-digest foods that promote the clarity and calmness which are vital to meditation.

In addition, you will soon begin to notice that alcohol and any mood or mind-altering substances you have been using, may cause a significant interference in your meditation. No one who really understands meditation thinks that drugs are helpful in attaining a meditative state, because drugs agitate the body and distract the mind through their toxic effects. Alcohol can create a sluggish, drowsy, dull-minded state that is an obstacle to meditation. Most people find that their interest in such experiences changes as they become increasingly drawn to the peace and quiet of meditation.

Sleep, like food, is a physical process that may also have a significant influence on your meditation. Too little sleep will make you drowsy and you may have difficulty remaining awake in meditation. However, too much sleep can be equally disruptive, creating a state in which you are sluggish, groggy or unable to concentrate.

Sleep is a fascinating process, which is very interesting to examine and observe as you learn to meditate. Generally speaking, as your meditation deepens, your need for sleep decreases, because meditation creates a deep, restful state for both body and mind.

As you progress in your meditative practice and it becomes more important to you, you will want to find ways to meditate at a time that allows you to be alert and fresh. Increasingly, it becomes a priority to plan circumstances in your life so that food, sleep, and other activities support your meditation, rather than interfere with your meditative practice.

3

Meditative Postures

A s indicated earlier, meditation is a simple technique
that almost everyone can enjoy. To meditate, you
simply sit quietly and comfortably in a relaxed and steady
position. You still the body, make the breathing process
serene, and then allow the mind to become quiet and
focused. We will clearly and systematically discuss these
three aspects of the meditative process—first, how we
position the body so that it is relaxed, steady, and
comfortable; next, why it is important to create a serene,
quiet breathing process and how to accomplish that; and
finally, how the mind is stilled and focused so that
meditation itself can take place. These three stages are a
movement from the most external, physical level to the
most subtle level. We will begin by considering the body
position and the process of meditation.

Sitting Postures for Meditation

The requirements for a good meditation posture are that it be still, steady, relaxed, and comfortable. If the body moves, sways, twitches or aches, it will distract you from meditation. Some people have the misconception that to meditate, you must sit in a complicated, cross-legged position called the "lotus pose." Fortunately, this is not accurate; there is actually only one important prerequisite for a good meditation posture, and that is, it must allow you to keep the head, neck, and trunk of the body aligned so that you can breathe freely and diaphragmatically.

Position of the Head, Neck, and Trunk

In all the meditative postures, the head and neck should be centered, so that the neck is not twisted or turned to either side, nor is the head held too far forward. The head should be supported by the neck and held directly over the shoulders without creating any tension in the neck or shoulders. Face forward, with your eyes gently closed. Simply allow the eyes to close and do not create any pressure in the eyes. Some people have unfortunately been told to try to force their gaze upward at a point in their forehead. This position creates strain and tension in the eyes and may even produce a headache. There are some yogic practices that involve specific gazes, but they are not used during meditation. Simply let all the facial muscles relax. The mouth should also be gently closed, without any tension in the jaw. All breathing is done through the nostrils.

Position of the Shoulders, Arms, and Hands

In all the meditative positions, your shoulders and arms are relaxed and allowed to rest gently on the knees, as you will see in the illustrations. Your arms should be so completely relaxed, that if someone were to pick up your hand, your arm would be limp. You can gently join the thumb and index fingers in a position called the "finger lock." This *mudra* or gesture creates a circle, which you may think of, symbolically, as a small circuit that recycles energy within, rather than extending your energy outward.

Sitting Positions for Meditation

There are many positions that allow you to keep the spine aligned and to sit comfortably without twisting your legs or creating any discomfort. In fact, the arms and legs are not really important in meditation. What is important is that the spine be correctly aligned. The easiest way to accomplish this is a posture called *Maitri asana* or Friendship Pose (see photograph on p. 32).

The photograph shows that in *Maitri asana*, you sit comfortably on a chair or bench, with your feet flat on the floor and your hands resting quietly in your lap. *Maitri asana* can be used by anyone, even those who are not very flexible or comfortable sitting on the floor. This posture allows you to begin the process of meditation

FRIENDSHIP POSE *(Maitri asana)*

without creating any difficulties for the body.

Easy Pose (Sukhasana)

If you are somewhat more flexible, you may want to begin sitting in an alternative position, called Easy Pose or *Sukhasana* (see photo, p. 34). In Easy Pose, you sit in a simple, cross-legged position on the floor or a platform. As you can see from the photograph, in Easy Pose each foot is placed on the floor under the opposite knee and the knees rest gently on the opposite foot. Fold a thick blanket underneath yourself so that your knees or ankles do not receive too much pressure. Your meditation seat should be firm, but neither too hard nor shaky. The seat should not be so high that it disturbs your body position.

If your legs are less flexible or your thigh muscles are tight, you may find that your knees remain fairly far off the floor. The suggestions for making sitting postures more comfortable will help you, and several warm-up stretching postures will also be beneficial in developing greater flexibility, increasing your comfort. Whatever position you select, practice it regularly and avoid frequent attempts at new postures—if you work regularly with developing one sitting posture it will become comfortable and steady over time.

EASY POSE *(Sukhasana)*

The Auspicious Pose *(Swastikasana)*

The Auspicious Pose, *Swastikasana* (see photo, p. 36), offers several advantages for those who can sit in it comfortably. If your legs are fairly flexible, you may actually find it more comfortable than Easy Pose, for longer periods of meditation. Because the position has a different, wider foundation, it distributes the body weight more directly on the floor, and is somewhat steadier and less likely to lead to swaying or other bodily movements.

As you can see in the illustration, in *Swastikasana*, the knees rest directly on the floor, rather than on the feet. One advantage of this posture for some students is that the ankle bones also receive less weight or pressure.

To develop the Auspicious Pose, you begin by sitting comfortably on your meditation seat, and you then bend the left leg at the knee and place the left foot alongside the right thigh. The sole or bottom of the left foot may be flat against the inside of the right thigh. Next, the right knee is bent, and the right foot is placed gently on the left calf, with the bottom of the foot against the thigh. The outside surface of the right foot is gently placed between the thigh and the back of the left calf, tucking in the toes. Finally, with your hand, you gently bring the toes of your left foot up between the right thigh and calf, so that the big toe is now visible. This creates a very symmetrical and stable posture, which is very effective for meditation. While the above description may sound complicated, you will find that if you follow the directions, it is not difficult.

AUSPICIOUS POSE *(Swastikasana)*

Finding Your Own Comfortable Position

For some beginning students, Auspicious Pose may not be comfortable initially because they lack flexibility in their legs. You can certainly sit in any individual variation of a cross-legged pose that allows you to be steady and keep the body still without jerkiness or swaying, or you may begin, as we said earlier, with *Maitri asana.* The important point is worth repeating: *It is more important to keep the head, neck, and trunk correctly positioned, so that the spine is aligned, than to put your legs in some particular position.*

Some students become very competitive with others about "advanced" positions, but may actually sit poorly because they hunch their shoulders over, creating a curve or bend in their spine. This is a very bad habit to develop, as it will create physical discomfort for you and obstruct your breathing, as well as interfere with the subtle energy channels of your body that are important in deeper meditation.

Problems with Back Muscles

Modern people tend to have poor posture because of the bad habits they have developed in walking and sitting. Because of this, the muscles that are meant to support the spinal column are underdeveloped, and the spine tends to curve with age, distorting the body. When you first begin sitting in meditation, you may notice that your back muscles are weak and that after a few minutes of sitting, you tend to slump forward.

Actually, this problem can be solved in very little time if you begin to pay attention to your posture throughout the day while sitting, standing, and walking. Adjust your posture when you notice that you are slumping. In this way, the back muscles will begin to do their job appropriately. The hatha yoga postures called the cobra, boat, bow, and child's pose will also be helpful in strengthening your back muscles so that they support the spinal column.

Some students with poor posture ask if they can do their meditation leaning back against a wall for support. In the beginning, you can do this to develop a correctly aligned posture or to check your alignment, although it is not good to remain dependent on such support. From the start it is best to work consciously and attentively with your posture. Ask a friend to check your posture or examine your posture while watching sideways in a mirror. If the spinal column is correctly aligned, you will not feel the knobs of the spinal vertebrae jutting out while you run your hand up your back.

Other Meditation Asanas (Postures)

Several other positions are popularly considered to be appropriate for meditation. We will briefly discuss some of the issues relating to these postures.

Thunderbolt Pose (Zen Sitting Position)

Some people who have had hip or knee problems may

have difficulty in the crosslegged sitting positions. They have suggested sitting on the legs with the hips over the ankles, in a position that has been known as "thunderbolt pose."

Unfortunately, trying to sit directly on the floor in this position places excessive strain on the feet and ankles, and may cause problems with the muscles or nerves. If you prefer to try to sit in this kind of position, it is better to use one of the wooden "Zen benches" that are commercially available. The student then sits directly on the bench or seat, removing the weight from the ankles and feet. There are still some limitations to the benefits of this position, because the posture may tend to be less stable for longer meditations, and it is more likely to allow the body to sway or move sideways. For some students, however, physical limitations may make this the best position.

Accomplished Pose (Siddhasana)

Traditionally, Siddhasana was taught to certain advanced students, although it is not presently recommended as a posture for general use. This is because, like the Lotus Pose, Siddhasana requires the ability to put the body into a particular position that is only helpful if it is done precisely and correctly. If one does not have the ability to completely attain the posture comfortably, it does not bring about the intended benefits and can, instead, create some difficulties or disturbances for the student. Siddhasana was not a position recommended for

ACCOMPLISHED POSE *(Siddhasana)*

beginners or those who intended to live in the world.

However, those who are adepts, or who have decided to lead a deep meditative life, should gradually learn to sit in this posture. Those who have decided to attain samadhi, particularly, should practice this posture during meditation. The posture is called the Adept or Accomplished Pose, and advanced students of meditation seek to form the habit of sitting in this posture, thus accomplishing their goal. When an advanced student can sit in this pose for more than three hours at a time, without any aches or pains, then *asana siddhi* is acquired. However, for beginners who are not yet ready, it is not necessary to put their bodies in a position in which they will be uncomfortable. Trying to sit in a position for which one is unprepared can result in injuries due to pulled muscles or ligaments.

In *Siddhasana*, (see photograph) the left heel is placed at the perineum (the region between the anus and the genitals) after the root lock has been applied. (This is done by contracting the anal sphincter muscles and pulling them in.) Now the other heel is placed at the pubic bone above the organ of generation. The feet and legs are arranged so that the ankle joints are in one line, or touch each other. The toes of the right foot are placed between the left thigh and calf so that only the big toe is visible, and the toes of the left foot are pulled up between the right thigh and calf so that the big toe is visible. The hands may then be placed on the knees.

We do not presently recommend this posture, except to those who learn it under direct personal guidance, because it can create difficulties for a student if incorrectly done. Traditionally this position was taught to men who intended to live as monks; however, it is false to think that men alone can sit in this posture. Women meditators and monks do sit in and practice this posture, although it may be less convenient.

The Lotus Pose

Like *Siddhasana*, the lotus pose (*Padmasana*) is generally not recommended for meditation, because unless it is applied precisely and correctly, its benefits do not occur—and almost no one can really sit absolutely correctly and comfortably in this posture, because it is difficult to maintain some other practices, called the *bandhas* (or locks) while in this position.

The Lotus Pose is a good exercise position, but advanced yogis and meditators use only the Accomplished Pose or *Siddhasana*. The Lotus Pose is a symbolic position, as the lotus is a symbol of the yogic life, which means learning to live in the world yet remain unaffected and above.

Presently, *Padmasana* is taught as an exercise to make the lower extremities limber and supple, rather than used for actual meditation, because for most students, sitting in this position is too uncomfortable to allow concentration. Since pain and discomfort prevent most students from meditation, we recommend that students sit in a posture that is steady and also comfortable.

In summary, for most students, using one of the first

three positions will allow you to make the most steady, consistent progress. Cultivate one position and regularly use it for meditation. If you do this, you will find that it becomes increasingly comfortable, steady, and still.

Suggestions for Making Sitting Positions More Comfortable

Most people will find it easiest to sit on the floor if they use a folded blanket to provide a padding for the entire area. Then, use a thick cushion or pillow under the buttocks and hips alone, supporting that part of the body off the floor three to four inches. Elevating the buttocks in this manner seems to relieve much of the pressure on the hip joints and knees, and you may be amazed what a difference it makes. Using a thick cushion under your buttocks will also make it easier to keep your spine correctly aligned.

As you become more flexible and comfortable, you may find that you can use a thinner cushion and eventually sit flat on the floor. However, it is important to keep the spine aligned and not allow it to curve over, disturbing your posture. At first, some people find it difficult to maintain this alignment without a thick cushion. Be patient in developing your sitting posture; you will find your body gradually becomes more flexible and can sit for longer periods more comfortably.

Stretching exercises and hatha yoga asanas can be very beneficial in helping you to make the body more flexible and comfortable in meditation. For further information or help with hatha practices, you may want to take a hatha yoga class, or see *Manual of Hatha Yoga*.[1]

Why Not Meditate Lying Down?

There are several reasons why it is not recommended that you meditate while lying down. One of the most important reasons is that most people rapidly fall asleep in a reclining position, and have difficulty maintaining any alertness or awareness. Obviously, if you are dozing or asleep, you won't be able to meditate.

Actually, there is also a more subtle and advanced reason: at deeper levels of meditation, it is important to be able to sit with the spine correctly aligned because this allows a certain type of energy to move upward through the body. This subtle and interesting topic is dealt with in detail in several advanced books on meditation, such as *Path of Fire and Light*.[2]

1. *Manual of Hatha Yoga I*, by Samskriti and Veda, is available from Himalayan Publishers.

2. *Path of Fire and Light*, by Swami Rama is also available from Himalayan Publishers.

4

Meditation, the Mind, and Mantra

Once you know how to sit in a meditative posture, you will probably wonder what exactly you do mentally as you seek to meditate. People wonder if they should try to think certain specific thoughts, or if they should try to make the mind completely empty, or if they should just let the mind drift and let associations flow into the mind. Actually, meditation does not involve any of these alternatives!

Thinking is a very different process than meditation, and, as we noted earlier, even contemplating an inspiring ideal, such as the concept of peace, is a different process. Trying to "make" anything happen in the mind in meditation is fruitless—you will simply become frustrated and irritated because the mind seems to fight attempts to control it. The motivation to strive or achieve is actually

45

of very little help in meditation. It's usually better not to create pressure for yourself about how your meditation should be or what you expect from the practice of meditation. Ironically, the *less* you strive or fight with yourself, the more you *allow* yourself to relax and achieve greater stillness, which is what "progress" in meditation means.

Similarly, it will not really work to try to make the mind "empty." By its very nature, the mind changes, processes memories, makes associations, and seeks to take in new information. In fact, the only time our minds usually become even somewhat still is in the state of deep, dreamless sleep. The rest of the time the mind tends to drift like a sailboat without an anchor.

Because of these mental processes, many meditative traditions seek to focus and quiet the mind by allowing the mind to concentrate on one object or stimulus at a time. Thus, the goal is not to make the mind empty, but rather, to quiet the mind by giving it one focus. In many meditative traditions, a word, phrase, sound or symbol is used to give the mind this one-pointed focus on which to concentrate. Some meditative disciplines favor the use of visual symbols, while in our tradition, the emphasis is on the use of a *mantra*—a word, sound, or set of words that one uses to give the mind an object of concentration.

Concentration is an important prerequisite for meditation. When we popularly use the word *concentration*, we sometimes imply a sense of effort to think or analyze, a process that may even sound a little stressful. However, the word concentration, as we mean it here, certainly does not imply effort, tension or mental strain—it simply means "focused attention." This focused attention is in contrast to a scattered, distracted state of mind. Concentration means an alert, yet relaxed focus of attention, and if you are relaxed and comfortable, this kind of concentration should not be difficult. When you cannot concentrate, it means that your ability to choose to direct the flow of your mind has been impaired. Many yogic techniques aid in the development of concentration, and will be discussed in detail later on. For now, it is simply important to understand that concentration is a prelude to meditation.

Many meditative traditions use mantras. For example, the words *Amen, Shalom,* and *Om* are all mantras. These mantras are mentally heard from within, rather than spoken or heard with the external auditory sense. A mantra is mentally heard during meditation rather than uttered aloud. The science of mantras is a particular and unique discipline and area of study; these sounds are not used lightly or trivially. Mantras are special sounds that have particular characteristics and effects, and not just any word can be a mantra.

Sounds vibrate and have no literal meaning, therefore they are known only through their vibrations. When they affect material substances, these vibrations create forms and their forms have names. Yet, actually, all the forms and names have come out of the sound vibrations themselves. There are certain sounds that vibrate in silence and are very powerful and beneficial in their effect on the entire human being. In ancient times the sages devoted their entire lives to meditation and heard these sounds, which are now used as mantras. Such sounds have different effects on different aspirants; a mantra is like a prescription that is given to a patient by a physician.

There are numerous sounds, syllables or words which have their effects on different levels. As far as the use of words is concerned, every word has a meaning, and when you use a word or mantra, the meaning should be associated with the meditator's level of feeling. An aspirant allows the word or mantra that is imparted to become part of his or her life. Many students try to coordinate the mantra with their breath; however, not all mantras are intended to be coordinated with the breath. There are a few mantras which can create jerks or a rhythm in the breath that could be injurious to the motion of the lungs and thus, the heart and brain. Therefore, do not try to coordinate all mantras with the breathing. The sounds that are coordinated with the breath include *So Hum, Om,* and *Omkar,* but other mantras should not be coordinated with breathing.

Mantras should be imparted by experienced, competent teachers only. Reading books and picking up mantras from books is not at all helpful. The technique of how to use a particular mantra is imparted directly to the student by the teacher. The most important point is the understanding of how to convey and appropriately use a particular mantra, otherwise the benefits of the practice may not occur. Ultimately, mantra is a powerful tool—a compact prayer. Constant prayer creates awareness and constant awareness leads to Self-realization.

In the modern world, the science of mantra is difficult to understand, because we have come to believe that anything that has value or truth can be uttered in words. Mantras operate at a deeper level; a mantra has its effect because of its qualities of sound and vibration rather than its literal meaning. Meaningfulness is a property of words, yet the goal in meditation is not to deal with the normal thinking, analyzing aspect of mind, but instead, to experience ourselves on other, deeper and more profound levels. This entire science of meditation and mantra is fascinating and the interested reader may want to continue his or her study of the use of mantra in meditation.

In summary, however, we will point out that all sounds have certain qualities—some sounds are soothing, some are energizing. The goal of the sounds we call mantras is to help to focus the mind so that we attain a deeper experience than that created by thinking alone.

While many traditions use mantras, in our tradition, we encourage students to begin by using the natural and universal sound that is pronounced *So Hum*. This sound is a general practice and can be used by most students. The sound is used in a particular way: As you sit quietly in meditation, you calm and quiet the breathing. You let your breathing become slow, smooth, and regular. Then, you allow your mind to mentally "hear" the sound *So Hum*. The first part, the softer sound, *So*, is heard with the inhalation, while the second part, *Hum*, is mentally heard during the exhalation. You simply sit quietly and let the sound repeat itself with each breath, allowing the breath flow to remain serene.

There are several important points to note here. The first is that the mantra is only heard mentally; it is not repeated aloud or with the mouth and vocal apparatus. As you continue to allow the mantra to repeat itself, you may find that the mind will create fewer distractions. In our normal waking awareness, mental activity usually consists of chains of associations or related thoughts and feelings. Some of these are intentional or goal-oriented, while some simply seem to "pop up" in our minds. In meditation, as we allow the mental noise to still itself, we keep the mind focused on the sound, *So Hum.* You will note that other thoughts do come to mind, and your awareness will shift to other issues. When this occurs, you allow yourself to "witness" or observe the association in the mind, and then you gently bring your awareness back to the sound *So Hum.*

It is important not to create a mental tug-of-war about this process: when thoughts arise in the mind, you simply "witness" them and bring the mind back to the sound, *So Hum.* In this way the meditation will deepen most easily. It is not helpful to engage in mental arguments or become angry or judgmental with ourselves about the mental distractions. Such emotional reactions consume even more energy. Thoughts will continue to arise, but most will dissipate if you witness them in a neutral way, without creating an internal conflict.

This process of "witnessing" is different from suppressing or repressing thoughts, because you are not seeking to keep certain kinds of thoughts from occurring or coming to consciousness. When they do occur, however, you notice their existence without elaborating upon them or intensifying them.

It is important to remember that not all mantras can be coordinated with the breathing in quite this way. In fact, you actually want to first calm and relax the breathing and then let go of that awareness. Your goal is not to keep on paying attention to the process of breathing itself. Most mantras will not coordinate with the exhalation/inhalation rhythm, and if you try to force the mantra to follow the breathing rhythm, you will create a distraction for yourself and disrupt your breathing. However, *So Hum* can be used effectively as a practice for almost everyone.

It is equally important to understand that as your meditation progresses, you may want to expand your mantra practice by receiving a personal mantra from a qualified teacher. These practices should be given personally by someone who is himself or herself qualified to do so—mantra practices should not be simply self-prescribed from books. Mantras do have powerful effects, but in order for a student to obtain the benefits, the practice must be appropriate for the student's level of experience. This can be determined by a competent teacher who is trained to impart these practices.

The mantra *So Hum*, like all mantras, has its effect because of the way sound affects us. While we might literally translate *So Hum* as "I am That," it is not due to the meaning of these words that the mantra has its impact. It is the effect of the sound that helps the mind to become still and eventually go beyond sound, to experience the silence within.

Sometimes students who come from religious backgrounds worry that their mantra should "come from" that tradition. As we said earlier, mantra as a technique is used in many traditions, but mantra itself is not a religious process. A qualified teacher, however, will be able to help you to work with a practice that does not create resistance or a sense of conflict within your own mind. *So Hum* does not belong to any religion. It is a pure technique that helps to quiet and focus the mind.

At first, when you are able to sit in meditation for only a few minutes, you will find that your mind may be somewhat distracted and noisy. However, as you create greater mental and physical stillness by paying attention to the foods you eat, the breathing process, and the kinds of mental influences you take in, you will find that the mental noise and distractibility tend to reduce. When you can gradually increase the length of your meditation, you may also notice that the mind tends to slow down and become quieter as the session of meditation progresses. In the chapter on breathing we will specifically address the link between mental serenity and the breathing process.

To sum up, the actual technique of meditation is very simple—you sit quietly, allow the breath to become even, and allow the mind to become calm and quiet. You attend to the mantra arising within yourself, and you keep bringing your mind back to the mantra when it wanders. While this process is not hard to describe, you may find it challenging to accomplish, because the mind is agile and tends to maintain a certain level of internal chatter. Often, we are not even aware of how noisy the mind is until we begin the practice of meditation. Our goal is to allow the noise to still itself. In part, we do this by letting go of things that create noise, conflict or mental turmoil.

The issue of "progress" in meditation becomes an important question for many people. In most of our activities, we can reassure ourselves that we are making progress by observing the external aspects of our behavior. We notice that we can go farther, faster or can do something in a larger or longer way. Meditation, however, presents a new situation: we cannot simply equate sitting for longer periods of time with meaningful progress in meditation. Sometimes we may sit for a long time, but our minds are scattered, distracted, and anything but peaceful.

Because of this insecurity about progress, and the question of whether one is "doing it correctly," some people become the victims of a kind of sensationalized view of meditation: that is, they think that if their meditation is going well, they should have some dramatic mental experiences such as perceiving visions, lights or colors. The simple truth is that, as meditation progresses, there should be a deepening sense of quiet and stillness— no dramatic phenomena are required.

Some people may experience physical sensations— twinges, twitches, or other kinds of impressions, but these generally indicate that there is tension that has been overlooked somewhere in the body, or else they indicate the presence of mental and emotional reactions that should not be mistaken for the experiences of deeper states of consciousness. Whatever phenomenal experiences arise, the student is encouraged to let them pass and keep his or her attention focused on the mantra, which will slowly and gradually take you to deeper levels of experiencing your own inner nature.

As your meditation practice becomes deeper, you will also probably become aware that certain types of experience lead to distractions in meditation. If you observe the kinds of experiences that preoccupy your mind, you will generally find that pleasant, happy feelings seldom create problems, although negative emotions or cravings can demand so much attention that all your mind wants to do is obsess on some negative or unpleasant experience.

At this point, we begin to notice that the kinds of thoughts we have and the experiences we seek out create either inner peace or inner chaos. This opens up a whole new area of observation and spiritual development—we seek to live our lives in such a way that we do not constantly create unpleasant experiences that dominate our minds or tie up our mental energy. This goal of creating experiences that lead to harmony and stillness is a very valuable aspect of preparing for meditation. We become increasingly aware of what kinds of experiences facilitate or disrupt our meditation later in the day.

In this sense, the meditator really becomes an internal explorer and investigator, who is studying the internal reactions and processes of his or her own mind, on both the conscious and unconscious levels. The meditator is an interior researcher, and what is brought out is creative intelligence that can be used in the external world. Meditation helps you to fully know and understand all the capacities of the mind—memory, concentration, emotion, reasoning, and intuition. Those who meditate begin to understand how to coordinate, balance, and enhance all these capacities, using them to their fullest potential. Then they go beyond the usual states of mind and consciousness through the practice of meditation.

As you begin to observe the beneficial effects of meditation on your body, mind, and the whole of your personality, you may become interested in still deeper practices and techniques that are a part of the system of meditation. If you sincerely and conscientiously do your meditation practice, you will definitely perceive many gradual changes. Don't give up in impatience or laziness; you will make steady progress if you continue your practice.

5

Breathing Practices

B reath awareness is an essential part of the practice of meditation, yet it is often misunderstood or underestimated by beginners. The most well-established schools of meditation teach breath awareness before teaching students advanced techniques of meditation, but some modern schools of meditation and relaxation do not understand the importance of breath awareness. In the practice of meditation, we first learn to still our bodies and then we become aware of physical twitches, tremors, and movements. Next, we begin to learn the techniques of breath awareness and we become aware that we can develop conscious control over the body, breath, and mind.

All of the exercises of breath awareness or breath control are part of the science of *pranayama*, which helps the student to regulate the motion of the lungs. Without such regulation, the respiratory system, the heart, the brain, and the autonomic nervous system do not function in a coordinated way, and disturbances in these physical processes limit progress in meditation.

Understanding the role of *pranayama* practices is important. *Prana* is a word that means "the first unit of energy," a subtler level of energy within the human being, which is the link between the body and the mind. Pranayama practices allow the student to channel and balance the flow of this subtle energy, which is responsible for the well-being and coordination of all the body's functions.

Whenever any emotional shock or strain is experienced in life, you can immediately observe its effect on the body by noticing how the breathing process changes. When we are shocked or surprised, we may hold the breath; when we are anxious or stressed, the breathing process becomes rapid and shallow. The process of breathing reflects the state of the mind at all times.

When our lives are chronically stressful, we may develop the habit of rapid, shallow breathing, which further disturbs the body and agitates the mind. In fact, the more rapid and shallow the breathing, the more difficult it is to think clearly or allow the mind to become quiet. Thus, the breathing process can have a powerful effect on the depth of our meditation.

Learning about the science of breath and how to work with the breath is vital for anyone who wants to learn advanced techniques of meditation. Once we have learned to sit in a quiet place in a comfortable, steady posture, and gross physical tension or tremors are no longer a source of disturbance, we may notice four irregularities in the breath. These are shallowness of breath, jerks in the breath, noisy breathing, and extended pauses between inhalation and exhalation. These problems create disturbances in the mind and prevent concentration, and these symptoms need to be eliminated to allow meditation to deepen.

In the ancient tradition of meditation, teachers did not impart the advanced techniques of meditation until they had determined that the student had attained stillness of the body and serenity of the breath. Sitting still is very important—the less movement, the more steady the mind will be. All of the movements, gestures, tremors, and twitchings of the body are caused by an undisciplined and untrained mind. When we observe our behavior, we find that there is not a single act or gesture that is independent of the mind. The mind moves first, and then the body moves, and the more the body moves, the more the mind dissipates.

The Science of Breath

The breath is the bridge or link between the body and the mind. Inhalation and exhalation are like two guards or sentries in the city of life, and their behavior changes instantly according to our thinking and emotions. Inhalation and exhalation are the "vehicles" through which the pranas—the vital force—travel in the body.

The sages observed that the breath is a kind of barometer, which registers the conditions of the mind and the influence of the external environment on the body. For example, the breath can warn us of impending illnesses that might create disturbances in the body.

Patanjali, the codifier of yoga science, explains that we can coordinate and quiet the mind by practicing the science of breath. According to our school of meditation, after we have established a still and comfortable posture, breath awareness is the next important step. Breath awareness allows us to create an undisturbed and joyous mind. When the breath begins to flow freely and smoothly through both nostrils, the mind attains a state of joy and calmness. Such a mental condition is necessary to allow the mind to travel into deeper levels of consciousness, for if the mind is not brought to a state of joy, then it cannot remain steady, and an unsteady mind is not fit for meditation.

When one starts to meditate on the flow of the breath, he or she can observe the four defects in its flow— noise, shallowness, jerkiness, and that which disturbs us the most, an extended pause between inhalation and exhalation. Much has been spoken about this in the meditative scriptures, but practice makes us increasingly aware of its importance. When one begins to meditate on the flow of the breath, one notices that such a pause distracts the mind, and thus, it is important to learn pranayama practices that allow us to eliminate these problems. Those who do not want to do pranayama exercises can still do meditation, but without breath awareness a deep state of meditation is impossible.

The breath and the mind are interdependent; if the breath is irregular and jerky, the mind is dissipated. After one attains steadiness in one's posture, then meditation on the breath and breath awareness become very natural. Breath awareness strengthens the mind and makes it easier for the mind to become inward. It is advisable for beginners to start by simply becoming aware of the breath. This is the simplest, most natural, and most essential step for attaining the deeper state of meditation.

Those students who are prepared for an advanced meditation technique realize the importance of breath awareness. When the mind begins to follow the flow of the breath, one becomes aware of the Reality, that there is a link between oneself and the center of the cosmos, which supplies breath to all living creatures. As long as the body receives the vital force, or prana, through the breath, the body/mind relationship is sustained. When this connection is disrupted, the conscious mind fails, and the body is separated from the inner unit of life. This separation is called death.

Breath awareness enables us to experience deeper levels of consciousness that cannot normally be experienced. In fact, you really cannot develop a deeper state of consciousness without working systematically with the breath. Thus, the first step in this process is the development of breath awareness.

Most of the time we are totally unaware and unconscious of the breathing process. The goal is to turn the attention and awareness to the flow of the breath itself, noticing how the breath flows, its quality of smoothness, from where in the body the breath seems to occur, and finally, the rhythm of the breath itself.

For example, you may notice that you breathe with the mouth ajar or that your breathing process is rapid, shallow, and irregular, or that the breath makes noise. The goal is to reestablish the body's natural respiratory pattern, which is called even, diaphragmatic breathing. In this normal breathing pattern, all inhalations and exhalations flow through the nostrils rather than the mouth, and the entire process is silent and noiseless. If you are breathing rapidly and shallowly, you are probably "chest breathing," which means that you are not allowing your breathing to be full and complete, and you are probably only using part of the lungs' capacity to inhale and exhale. When you establish diaphragmatic breathing, you allow the lungs to expand fully with the inhalation and to be emptied more completely on exhalation.

When you breathe evenly and diaphragmatically, the breathing becomes more complete and efficient, so you will breathe more slowly, since each breath is more effective. However, it is impossible to breathe diaphragmatically unless the head, neck, and trunk of the body are correctly aligned. To understand this, it may be helpful to look at the diagram on page 63.

The lungs are actually very elastic and expansive, and when they are efficiently filled, their capacity is far greater than when we breathe shallowly, as in chest-breathing. The lungs are separated from the lower abdominal cavity by the diaphragm muscle, which moves up and down

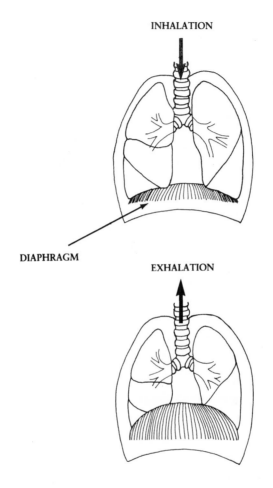

Movement of the diaphragm during inhalation and exhalation.

within the chest. As the diaphragm moves up, the lungs are emptied; as the diaphragm comes down, the lungs are allowed to fill more completely. You cannot really observe the diaphragm muscle, but when you breathe diaphragmatically, you may notice that the lower ribs flair out slightly on inhalation, and the abdominal area may also move out a bit. On exhalation, the abdominal area moves back in toward the spinal column.

If your posture is poor and your spine is curved you will be unable to breathe freely, and will unconsciously constrict the movement of diaphragmatic breathing, resulting, instead, in rapid, shallow breathing. This is one reason why sitting posture is so important: if the spine is poorly aligned, you cannot breathe freely, and when the breathing process is disturbed, the mind will become agitated.

The first step in diaphragmatic breathing is to become aware of posture, and to learn to be comfortable in an erect, correctly aligned position. This allows diaphragmatic breathing to develop. Then, you begin to notice whether the exhalations and inhalations are equal in length. While there are some breathing exercises that intentionally alter the length of the exhalations or inhalations, most people do this unconsciously, and this is damaging to the body.

One way to reestablish an even pattern is to mentally count the length of the inhalation and exhalation, allowing them to become equal. However, in counting the breath, you may notice that there is a tendency for you to hold or pause slightly as you think each number. A better way to do this is to exhale as if you were breathing down to the toes and inhale up to the crown of the head. It is important to keep the entire process even and smooth in flow, without any jerkiness or irregularity. At the conclusion of the smooth exhalation, you begin another inhalation, and continue on in this manner. If you begin to pay attention to the breathing process when you are not meditating you can learn to correct this problem, and then, when you meditate, the breath will be naturally smooth and even.

The next point is also very important. Many people unconsciously hold the breath between exhalation and inhalation. This is an extremely bad habit, because it tenses the body, disrupts the normal breathing rhythm, creates imbalance in the nervous system and, by throwing off a healthy respiratory rhythm, is said traditionally to be damaging to the heart. Eliminating this unconscious tendency to pause or hold the breath is a major goal. The entire breathing process should be smooth and natural, without any breathlessness, gasping, or feeling of being forced.

When the breath is smooth and there is no force or constriction, then the breath will naturally be silent. Noisy breath means either that you are using force or that there is some obstruction or congestion in the respiratory passages.

The breathing process has become fine and subtle when the breathing is deep, even, and diaphragmatic, the length of the exhalations and inhalations are equal, the breath is silent and noiseless, and finally, when there is no pause between the inhalation and the exhalation. When that occurs, meditation can go to a deeper level.

Because the stress and strain of daily life have distorted our natural breathing processes, most students will have to become aware of consciously reestablishing this normal process. At first, this will require attention, both during meditation and also during the day's other activities. Although most students do not want to be told this, you should actually plan to spend four weeks consciously attending to the breathing and learning how to breathe diaphragmatically before you turn your attention to other aspects of meditation.

There are several techniques that will help you to become aware of diaphragmatic breathing. First, you can lie on your back on the floor in the relaxation pose known as corpse posture. If you place one hand on the chest and the other on the abdomen, at about the navel area, it will be easy for you to become aware of when you are breathing diaphragmatically, because you will feel the gentle movement at the navel, as the abdomen rises with inhalation and falls with exhalation. If you are breathing diaphragmatically, you will not feel much movement in the chest.

You can also do a breath awareness practice in this position using a sand bag (weighing about 6-10 pounds) which is placed across the abdomen to help you develop diaphragmatic breathing. You simply lie in this position and pay attention to the movement of the abdominal area.

Lying on your stomach in the crocodile pose will also help you to become aware of and develop your diaphragmatic breathing. In the crocodile pose, you lie face down with your feet pointing outward. Put your forehead on your crossed forearms and breathe deeply. In this position it will be easy for you to feel the movement of the abdomen against the floor. Breathing and relaxing in this posture for 5-10 minutes, twice a day, morning and evening, can help you to make diaphragmatic breathing a habit. Once you can maintain diaphragmatic breathing during the day or when lying down, it will be normal to breathe this way while sitting upright in meditation.

2:1 BREATHING EXERCISE

When you have mastered diaphragmatic breathing, you will notice that your meditation changes. There are also several other practices that will be very helpful to you. The following practice, 2:1 Breathing, will help you to relax, eliminate waste gases from the body, and increase your stamina and endurance. You can do it while sitting or while walking, and you will find it very energizing.

In 2:1 Breathing, the exhalation is twice the length of the inhalation. For example, you may exhale to a count of eight, and then inhale to a count of four. In this exercise you do not hold the breath. Experiment with this exercise for five to ten minutes a day for two weeks and you will notice how much more energy you feel.

Pranayama and the Nervous System

The science of pranayama is closely connected with the autonomic nervous system. Pranayama techniques are intended to help balance the functioning of the nervous system, and bring these usually involuntary processes under conscious control. They are important preparatory practices for meditation, and if you experiment with them and observe their effects, you will find that they have significant benefits, calming and relaxing the body and stilling the mind.

Long before the modern knowledge of the nervous system, the ancient yogis were aware of the flow of prana energy through channels called *nadis*. Although these nadis are not the same as nerves, the nadis are the subtler coordinates of the physical nerves. There are thousands of nadis, but three main nadis play an important role: *ida*, *pingala*, and *sushumna*.

Sushumna is the central channel, and corresponds to the physical spinal column. The other two nadis, ida and pingala, are associated respectively with the left and right sides of the central column. Ida and pingala also originate at the base of the spine. Ida terminates in the left nostril, and pingala in the right. Normally, energy flows through these two side columns in alternation. The goal of many pranayama practices is to allow pranic energy to flow upward through the sushumna column, which creates a state of particular joy, serenity, and higher consciousness.

Modern physiological research has confirmed what the ancient yogis experienced long ago: The main flow of the breath shifts back and forth between the left and right nostrils. Although the average person might be surprised to discover it, one nostril is always more open and the breath flows more freely through it than through the other, more obstructed nostril. This more open-feeling nostril is called the active or dominant nostril, while the less open nostril is considered to be passive.

In a healthy person, this process of nostril dominance will shift about every ninety minutes to two hours, as the previously active and passive nostrils shift roles. The physiological process that makes this possible is fascinating: the tissues in the nasal passage on one side engorge with blood, becoming more full and slightly closing the airway. At the same time, the passages in the opposite side become more open, to allow a greater volume of flow.

If you want to determine which of your nostrils is presently active, it is very easy to do. You can simply exhale slowly through the nostrils and place your fingertips in the flow of the exhalation. The side from which you feel the greater and easier exhalation volume is the active or dominant nostril at this time.

If you have difficulty perceiving a difference, you can use a small pocket mirror to do a test: Place the mirror under your nostrils and notice the vapor pattern that condenses on the glass of the mirror. One pattern is usually somewhat larger, indicating the active nostril. Of course, even when your head is badly congested, neither side is ever really completely closed. As indicated, this pattern will shift every ninety minutes or so, so if you check later, it is likely that you will notice the opposite pattern.

In the ancient yogic texts, this is just the beginning of the science of breath, *Swarodaya*, an intricate and precise science that is very intriguing. As your interest in this amazing science deepens, you may want to study other texts, such as *Science of Breath*, or *Path of Fire and Light*, to deepen your understanding.

However, to return to the main point: The goal of the pranayama practice is to develop the skill to voluntarily control the respiratory processes, and to create a joyful, deep state of mind that is conducive to meditation, by learning to simultaneously open both nostrils. To learn to do this, a series of pranayama practices are taught, one of the most important of which is called *Nadi Shodhana*, or *Alternate Nostril Breathing*.

Alternate Nostril Breathing *(Nadi Shodhana)*

There are many variations on Alternate Nostril Breathing, and each has a particular purpose, but as the name implies, they all share the theme of alternating the flow of breath between the two nostrils. As your practice of Alternate Nostril Breathing advances, there are more subtle and extensive variations, including some that are done using retention of breath. In our tradition, however, we do not encourage students to begin with breath retention. Breath retention should not be done unless the student has a profound knowledge of *bandhas* (locks) and *mudras*, so only advanced students are taught retention. Retention intensifies the mind's focus, and if the mind is not serene and balanced, this may not be beneficial. Such experiments have been repeatedly conducted at the Institute's Dana Research Laboratory.

To learn Alternate Nostril Breathing is a simple

process and you will find that it is a very effective tool for helping to calm the nervous system and prepare the mind for meditation.

The first exercise of Alternate Nostril Breathing should be practiced for about two months, until it has been refined, and then more advanced variations may be added.

Nadi Shodhana is done sitting upright in a meditative posture. It is done after yogic asanas and relaxation, and it is a preparation for meditation. This practice should be done at least twice a day, morning and evening, as well as before meals. It is said to purify and balance the nadis, balance the flow of breath in the nostrils, and create a state of clarity and serenity that is suitable for meditation. It also seems to help balance the functioning of the autonomic nervous system.

FIRST METHOD OF ALTERNATE NOSTRIL BREATHING

1) In your seated meditative position, check the alignment of the head, neck and trunk, so that the spine is correctly positioned and you can breathe freely.

2) Determine which of the nostrils is active.

3) In this exercise, all the exhalations and inhalations should be of equal duration and should be smooth, slow, and controlled. Do not allow the breath to be forced or jerky. Allow the eyes to be gently closed.

4) A special hand position is used to gently close the nostrils in alternation: Bring the right hand up to the nose, and fold the index and middle fingers to the palm, so that you can gently use the right thumb to close the right nostril, or the ring finger to close the left. Be sure you are not bending over to bring the head down to the hand. Also be aware of how much pressure or force you use with the thumb or finger in closing the nostril. Very little pressure is needed. You can simply rest the thumb or finger against the side of the nostril; this does not require more than a touch.

5) To begin the practice, you gently close the passive nostril and exhale smoothly and completely through the active nostril.

6) At the end of the exhalation, you close the active nostril, release the passive nostril, and inhale through the passive nostril slowly and completely. The duration of the inhalation and exhalation should be equal and there should be no sense of forcing the exhalation or inhalation.

7) Repeat this cycle of exhaling through the active nostril and inhaling through the passive nostril two more times.

8) At the end of the third inhalation through the passive nostril, exhale through the same nostril, keeping the active nostril closed.

9) When this exhalation is completed, close the passive nostril, and then open the active, inhaling through the active nostril.

10) Repeat two more cycles, exhaling through the passive and inhaling through the active.

11) Place the hands on the knees and then exhale and inhale through both nostrils evenly for three complete breaths. This completes one set of the exercise.

FIRST METHOD OF
ALTERNATE NOSTRIL BREATHING

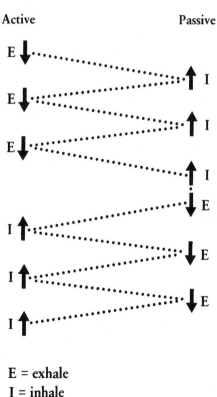

E = exhale
I = inhale

After you have worked with this exercise and achieved the ability to keep the exhalations and inhalations smooth, even, and noiseless, you will notice that the length of the inhalations and exhalations tends to increase. Allow yourself to progress in letting the process become slower, smoother, and more consciously focused. When you can do that, you are ready for the next level.

SECOND AND THIRD METHODS
OF ALTERNATE NOSTRIL BREATHING

At the intermediate level, students should practice three cycles of nadi shodhana. Exhale and inhale through both nostrils evenly for three complete breaths between cycles. Either three cycles of the first method, or one each of the three methods can be practiced. The second and third methods are listed below.

As you progress in this exercise you will want to give it more time and attention. Always keep the breath smooth and even. Do not force yourself to go beyond what is comfortable. There should not be any need to gasp or force the breath. Your goal is to achieve a subtle, smooth serenity in the breath.

These pranayama and breathing exercises can be practiced twice a day, and other breathing practices can also be done after doing physical postures. However, breath retention should be done only under the supervision of a competent guide who has practiced them and who trains the student in the use of bandhas and mudras.

SECOND METHOD OF
ALTERNATE NOSTRIL BREATHING

Active   Passive

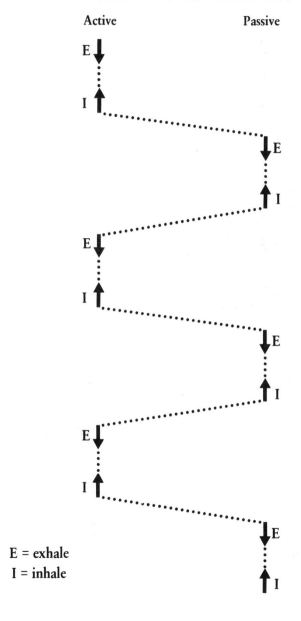

E = exhale
I = inhale

THIRD METHOD OF
ALTERNATE NOSTRIL BREATHING

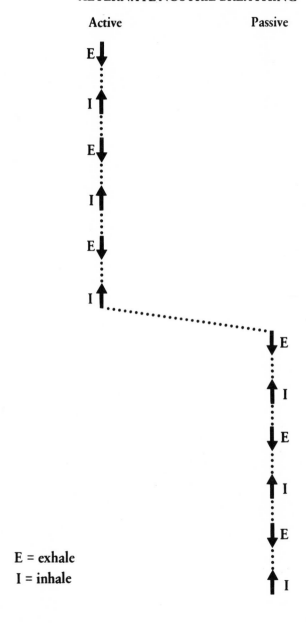

Active   Passive

E = exhale
I = inhale

Otherwise, a disturbance in the pranic vehicles can create breathing disorders that are injurious for the heart, brain, and other systems.

Breathing exercises are numerous, but we are teaching here a few subtle exercises, which help the student to apply *sushumna awakening*. Sushumna awakening is very important for the higher stages of meditation, in which the breath starts flowing freely in both nostrils. When this is achieved, a particular joy is realized and the mind does not roam around, but remains in a state of joy. Such a state of joyful mind makes one fit to meditate and attain the state of tranquility.

6

A Program for Progress in Meditation

This program is the result of thorough examination and experimentation by the tradition of the sages. Many sincere students of meditation have experienced its benefits. If you really want to attain the highest state of meditation, you should commit yourself to following this system, which is very simple:

a) Learn to sit at the same time every day, and allow this to become a habit.

b) Develop a good sitting posture for meditation. There are only a few postures that are really appropriate for meditation. These include *sukhasana, siddhasana,* and *swastikasana.* Choose one position and regularly practice that same position for meditation. The body will adjust accordingly.

Guidelines and Goals for the First Month

The first one or two months should be devoted to attaining a still, comfortable posture. Meditative posture should be steady and comfortable. Steadiness of posture means that you are able to sit still and can keep the head, neck, and trunk aligned. Allowing the posture to become comfortable means that you are not uneasy or disturbed in any way. The cushion that you use as a meditation seat should be neither too high nor too hard, and it should never be a spongy, unsteady cushion.

For the first month, you may use the support of a wall to help you tell when you are keeping your head, neck, and trunk in a straight line. After that, learn to sit independently of such support. A very good meditation seat can be made from a wooden plank or board covered with two blankets that are folded into quarters.

At the first level of practice, obstacles may arise on several dimensions: First, the body may shake, perspire or become numb. Next, the subtler muscles, such as the cheeks or eyes, twitch. One should learn to ignore all this. At first, the body rebels when you try to discipline it. If your throat gets dry while you are doing meditation, you can take a few sips of water. In certain cases, you may notice that there is excess saliva in the mouth. Both of these symptoms are unhealthy and may be due to over-eating or consuming bad food.

When you begin to sit in meditation, you should not try to sit for a long time. To start, 15-20 minutes will be sufficient. Every third day, you can expand your practice by three minutes. Gradually, when the posture becomes steady, the time will easily extend itself. Developing a still, steady posture will bring you great joy. Discomfort is not a good sign; massage your toes, legs, and thighs with your hands when you get up from your meditation seat.

Pray to the Lord that your meditation will continue to become better and will create the motivation to again sit in meditation, so that you await your meditation time with great desire. But remember that you are praying to the Lord of Life, who is seated in the inner chamber of your own being; this sort of prayer strengthens your awareness. Do not pray for anything else except to strengthen your meditation. Selfish prayers feed the ego and make the aspirant weak and dependent. Prayer should be God-centered and not ego-centered.

EXERCISE 1

As you begin your meditation, survey and observe your body mentally: your eyes are gently closed, your teeth are gently touching, your lips are sealed, and your hands are placed lightly on the knees.

Complete this survey of your body systematically, from the crown of the head downward. In the forehead, let there be no tension; in the cheeks and jaws, no tension; in the neck and shoulders, no tension. From the arms to the fingertips there should be no tension.

Mentally return to the shoulders, allowing no tension. Let there be no tension in the chest. Take several deep breaths when you begin and mentally surrender and let go. When you come to the chest, inhale and exhale within your comfortable capacity. This will help you to relax your body. Do not make suggestions to your body but rather, survey it and then let your attention move on to the abdominal area. Survey the pelvic area, the hips, thighs, knees, calves, ankles, and feet.

Now inhale and exhale at least five to ten times. Visualize your body and again systematically come back through the body in the same order, returning to the crown of the head. Survey your body thoroughly; if you find that a certain part of the body has any aches or pain, you can discover that and gently ask your mind to go to that spot to heal that aching part. The mind definitely has the inner capacity to correct and heal such discomfort; do not doubt that.

Understanding the Mind

The mind is the master of the body, breath, and senses, though it is, itself, charged by the power of the Center of Consciousness (the individual soul). All our thinking processes, emotional power, capacity for analysis, and the functioning of the different modifications of mind are due to the power of the soul. One simply has to become aware of this fact, that the mind is in direct control of the senses, breath, and body. It is the mind that influences the senses and causes them to function in the external world. It is the mind that desires to perceive the world through the senses and to conceptualize and categorize those sensory perceptions. The mind stores such impressions in the unconscious, the storehouse of merits and demerits, and then it recalls them whenever it needs them.

All *sadhanas* (spiritual practices), techniques, and disciplines are actually means to train the mind. And the foremost part of the training is to make the mind aware that Reality lies beyond itself, and that is the immortality of the soul. The mind is a separate, individual entity, but it does not have a separate existence; it exists only because of the existence of the soul.

The mind is the finest instrument that we possess. If it is understood well, the mind can be helpful in our sadhana; however, if the mind is not well-ordered and disciplined, it can distract and dissipate all our potentials.

Anything within the domain of the mind can be healed by the mind, once one knows his or her deeper nature. When the aspirant becomes aware of this fact, he or she can willfully heal or prevent the occurrence of those diseases that have their basis in malignancy.

There are four distinct functions of mind: *manas, buddhi, ahamkara,* and *chitta.* These four should be understood and their functioning should be coordinated. *Manas* is the lower mind, through which the mind interacts with the external world and takes in sensory impressions and data. Manas also has the tendency to doubt and question, which can cause great difficulties if this tendency becomes excessive.

Buddhi is the higher aspect of mind, the doorway to inner wisdom. It has the capacity to decide, judge, and make cognitive discriminations and differentiations. It can determine the wiser of two courses of action, if it functions clearly and if manas will accept its guidance.

Ahamkara is the sense of "I-ness," the individual ego, which feels itself to be a distinct, separate entity. It provides identity to our functioning, but ahamkara creates our feelings of separation, pain, and alienation as well.

Chitta is the memory bank, which stores impressions and experiences, and while it can be very useful, chitta can also cause difficulties if its functioning is not coordinated with the others. These functions are described in greater detail in *The Art of Joyful Living.*

Just as an aspirant should care for and pay attention to the different functions of mind (*manas, chitta, buddhi,* and *ahamkara*), which have different abilities and duties, so also should the student take care of his external behavior, so that he does not acquire the diseases that are transmitted through unhealthy food, sex, or imbalanced ways of living.

Cleanliness is valuable, but it should not become obsessive, because in order to function effectively, the immune system also requires a healthy mind. When we talk about purity of mind, that is actually achieved by ridding ourselves of negative, passive, and slothful mental tendencies. Such a healthy mind acquires self-confidence, and then *buddhi* judges, discriminates, and decides things on time.

To establish coordination among the various modifications of mind, one has to learn to watch the mind's functioning through our actions and speech, and at the same time, observe the thinking process within. Ignorance is the mother of all diseases, discomfort, pains, and miseries. A purified, quiet, and serene mind is positive and healthy. The process of meditation helps the mind to remain a useful and constructive instrument.

Such a clear mind, which has been trained to become purified and one-pointed, can in many cases also heal others. Self-healing is one of the natural physical capabilities and tendencies of each person's mind. For example, suppose that a person is peeling an apple and cuts his or her finger, so that it begins to bleed. You'll notice that the cells of the body act as if they have a kind of understanding, and they function in the cut to protect the injured and destroyed cells. In time, according to the health of the body's immune system, the body heals itself. But in a body whose mental and emotional processes are not coordinated, something may allow excessive cell growth there, and may eventually create a growth. Due to such a lack of coordination and balance at a subtle level of mental functioning, some diseases occur and disturb our sadhana.

I believe that if we become emotionally attached to the external objects of the world, but remain unable to unfold ourselves and our highest potential, then life is incomplete and we become victims of discontent and dissatisfaction. Therefore, a student should apply all his or her present resources to make the body, breath, senses, and mind into healthy tools, so that sadhana is accomplished.

When you attain a state of meditation, in which the body has become perfectly still and quiet, and it does not move, shake or tremble, and muscle twitches no longer occur, then there is a feeling of unusual joy, which is quite different from the other joys of worldly experience. Then you can begin to watch your breath, and develop the next state of meditation.

Remember that practicing Breath Awareness is very important and vital for meditation. Observe your breathing to see if you notice any problems with the four common faults we discussed earlier—jerkiness in the breath, shallowness, noise or extended pauses.

The body should be still, with the head, neck and trunk aligned, so that your breathing can flow smoothly.

Practice for the Second Month

In the second month, you can extend your practice as follows:

After you have done your stretching and limbering exercises, then do your breathing exercises. To relax the gross muscles, physical exercises are healthy, but to create a deeper level of relaxation in the subtle muscles and the nervous system, breathing exercises are even more helpful. Even Breathing and Alternate Nostril Breathing are very healthy preparatory practices, but during meditation itself, the only exercise that is recommended is Breath Awareness. Breath is one of the great focal points of the mind. The mind and the breath are inseparable associates, and it is easy and spontaneous for the mind to focus on the breath.

As we said earlier, in the beginning, for the first

month, the aspirant should focus the mind on the flow of the breath, watching and observing the breath and seeking to remove the four main problems with breath. In the next step of breathing practice, the mind should be carefully focused on the exercise described below.

EXERCISE 2

This will be a delightful experience for the student, but remember that you will experience this delightful and pleasant state only if you do not jump from an awareness of bodily posture to breath awareness. If you first learn to make the posture steady, still, and comfortable, this experience will become very delightful.

This particular exercise is very subtle; it is finer, more advanced, and more refined that the other experiences you have had in Breath Awareness. In our research laboratory, we have had extensive experience with this exercise and it has also been the focus of experiments done for thousands of years by a line of sages and teachers.

Inhale as though you are breathing from the base of the spine to the crown of the head, without creating any disturbances in the breath. Exhale as though you are exhaling to the base of the spine. It will be helpful if you can visualize three cords: in the center, the centralis canalis, and on the sides, ida and pingala. (Ida and pingala are two of the main nadis described earlier.)

Inhale and exhale through the centralis canalis, which is the finest, milky white tube. Feel the subtle current of

energy that flows between the medulla oblongata (at the base of the brain) and the pelvic plexus. Observe your mind and see how many times it becomes distracted. The moment the mind is distracted, you will find that there is a slight jerk or an irregularity in the breath. During this practice, it is recommended that you continue the gentle flow of the breath without jerks, noise, shallowness or extended pauses.

After you inhale and exhale with awareness of the spine, you next become aware of the breath as it comes and goes through the nostrils. You may notice that one nostril seems blocked and the other may seem to be more open. You can easily inhale through one but not the other. In such cases, pay attention to the blocked nostril, and you may be surprised to notice that in a few seconds' time, the blocked nostril has opened.

For example, in this manner you might first pay attention to the right nostril and when it has become open and easy to breathe through, you then pay attention to the other nostril, in order to open it. If you practice this systematically, it will not take you much time to develop control over the flow of the breath.

The breath and mind are twin laws of life: they are very close to each other and very easily influence each other. Although they both have a separate existence, they register each other's influence. We are trying to establish the awareness that the flow of the breath can be channeled by choice, through simple attention of mind. Soon you will find that the moment your thinking changes, the breath also switches.

After experimenting with the electrical potentials associated with both nostrils, the sages discovered that these two aspects of breath have different natures. Breathing through the left side has a cooling effect, while the right-sided breath has a warming effect.

According to this advanced Science of Breath, when you notice that one nostril is more active, during that time, one of the *tattvas* (subtle elements of the physical body) are active and one of them becomes most prominent, which of course creates a disturbance in the mind. This is what causes the alteration in the flow of the breath. The *tattvas,* or physical elements, are affected by the flow of the breath through the left and right nostrils, and vice versa. However, once you gain control over the breath, it can also give you control over the changes in the tattvas, according to your discrimination and concentration as a student of meditation. This is a profound science discussed in much greater detail in *Path of Fire and Light.*

Creating a Meditative State of Mind: Awakening Sushumna

Now, let us go on to the next step: the process of making the mind calm and joyous, so that the mind experiences delight in practicing meditation. This method is called *sushumna awakening.* The aspirant who has the patience to proceed according to this program will surely benefit. Those who are "economy readers" will probably read through this description without ever practicing it, and they will gain only a glimpse of this process. May God bless them and hopefully someday they will also walk on this path of light.

To begin the process of sushumna awakening, the meditator is prepared to focus the mind on the breath as it is felt between the two nostrils. Mind you, this is not a focus on the top of the nostrils; it is not *trataka* (an external gaze). The goal is to focus awareness on the flow of the breath, where it can be perceived at the nostrils on inhalation and exhalation. When you focus the mind on the center between the nostrils, you will soon discover that both nostrils are flowing freely. When both nostrils flow freely, that is called *sandhya,* the wedding of the sun and the moon, or between pingala and ida. This is a delightful moment, in which neither worry, fear nor other negative thoughts can distract the mind. However, it is important to realize that, because students do not have much experience and practice in creating this state, it does not usually last and is difficult to maintain for a very long time.

When one regularly prepares to focus the mind on the center between the two nostrils, morning and evening, he will find that the mind easily attains a state of joy. Then, the student becomes eager to again attain this joy and looks forward to his or her meditation all day. When both nostrils flow freely, it means that one is inhaling and exhaling through both nostrils simultaneously, which is the sign of sushumna awakening. Once this experience can be maintained for five minutes, the student has crossed a great barrier, and the mind has attained some one-pointedness. Then, the mind becomes focused inward. Two to three months should be devoted to this *kriya* or practice.

The Conscious Mind

The conscious mind is that part of mind which functions during the waking state. It is merely a small fragment of the totality of the mind. Our educational system—whether at home, in school or in the colleges and universities—has no systematic program that teaches us how to really understand and become aware of the whole of the mind, especially the unconscious mind. The small part of mind that is cultivated by our educational system, from our childhood onward, is merely the conscious mind.

The conscious mind employs and relies on ten senses to collect data for it from the external world of objects. These consist of five subtle cognitive senses (sight, hearing, taste, smell, and touch) and five gross active senses (the hands, feet, the power of speech, and the organs of reproduction and elimination.)

We commonly know only a little about how to educate the small conscious aspect of mind. The sages, however, with the assistance of deeper meditative methods, learned to dive deeply into the inner recesses of the unconscious mind and then, to make use of it and its capacities in an orderly way. These sages and great ones are able to accomplish that with a simple, systematic method of meditation. Most human beings continue to operate on or function barely above the level of the brute, because they do not know how to gain access into the deeper aspects of the mind. That is why we do not become aware of our deeper personalities.

There are many problems and obstacles to overcome, in order to help the ordinary mind to understand itself. The mind usually remains clouded, confused, and undisciplined in the external world, where everything seems to move and change. Because the mind itself is confused, even learning how to collect data correctly, or accurately perceive the external world, is a serious problem for the ordinary mind.

However, those who are meditators learn to purify the mind and make the mind one-pointed. For them, it then becomes possible to collect the data and impressions exactly as they are. Such a person sees things clearly, while in contrast, the clouded mind remains distorted and dissipated.

With the help of meditation, the conscious mind can be trained to form a new habit. The personality can be transformed when one learns to let go of the habitual thoughts arising in the conscious mind. Then, the next step is to learn to witness the thoughts going on in your mental train, practicing and learning to remain undisturbed, unaffected, and uninvolved. Another three to four months of regular meditative practice will allow you enough time to learn to deal with the conscious aspect of the mind.

Sometimes people feel that they have perfect control over their minds, but that is not accurate, because even if they control the conscious mind, they cannot control the unknown, unconscious mind, which is extensive. The unconscious is a vast reservoir of the impressions resulting from our deeds, actions, desires, and emotions. These latent, dormant levels of mind remain unknown to the aspirant. Even when the conscious mind has become seemingly calm, a single impression (such as a memory) that arises from the unconscious can suddenly distort the mind, exactly the way that a pebble's splash can disturb the smooth surface of a lake.

Human emotion is an immense power, which usually operates below the surface of the lake of mind, like a fish swimming under water. If that emotion is not guided, it can pollute and contaminate the whole lake of the mind. In this endeavor, students need to learn patience with themselves. Actually, our impressions, thought patterns, and emotions are identical to our own deeds, because a thought is virtually a deed.

To fear and try to escape from examining one's own thought processes is a serious mistake for a student to make. You should examine all your fears, and then you will find that most fears are imaginary and irrational. From this point, you then begin the process of contemplation with analysis. Gradually, you will acquire the power to inspect your own thinking process, while remaining undisturbed. Such a mind attains clarity and is then prepared to attain *samadhi*. There are many levels of samadhi, which is a state of deep, absorbed meditation. When a student can focus his or her mind for ten minutes without any disturbance, he or she has nearly attained this goal.

All human beings who are aware of the reality of life, and who have already examined the small joys and pleasures of the world, will realize that they cannot remain content or truly satisfied without practicing meditation. Meditation creates the highest of all joys; meditation creates fearlessness. Glory to the path of meditation!

The final step of meditation is to remain in silence. This silence cannot be described; it is inexplicable. This silence opens the door of intuitive knowledge, and then the past, present, and future are revealed to the student.

Once upon a time, a student of meditation went to see a sage. The student began discussing philosophical concepts, such as God and the divine existence, but the sage didn't say anything. The aspirant talked on and on about God and asked many probing questions, but still the sage kept still. Finally, in frustration, the aspirant inquired why the sage wouldn't answer his questions. Then the sage smiled and said gently, "I have been answering you, but you are not listening: God is silence."

In the course of my search and study in the Himalayas and the other parts of India, I met a fortunate few, who enjoyed such a deep state of silence and who also helped those who are prepared to meditate.

Beyond body, breath, and mind lies this silence. From Silence emanate peace, happiness, and bliss. The meditator makes that silence his or her personal abode; that is the final goal of meditation.

Om. Peace, Peace, Peace . . .

7

Questions and Answers on the Practice of Meditation

Q: Why isn't "meditation music" considered helpful in deepening meditation?

A: Music is an external stimulus, which takes your sensory system and mind in the direction of external awareness, rather than the inward focus of meditation. Concentration on some pleasant, external stimulus—such as a rose or music—can be quite soothing, but it doesn't lead you in the direction of the highest state of consciousness within. Enjoy music at other times, but do not confuse this with meditation.

Q: What about using incense or candles? Are they necessary or helpful?

A: For the same reason, burning incense while meditating isn't recommended, because the scent or smoke can prove to be a distraction. If you wish, burn a little incense before you meditate to establish a pleasant atmosphere, but we recommend you put the incense out when you begin to meditate.

Candles that flicker can also be quite a distraction, even though your eyes are gently closed. If you can obtain a good quality, non-flickering candle, you'll find it less bothersome, but again, since your focus is not meant to be on the candle, such external light is not essential.

Q: There seem to be many different meditative traditions and techniques. What accounts for these differences and how do I know which technique is best for me?

A: All authentic meditative traditions seek to help the student know his or her own most essential nature. These seemingly different techniques can be compared to many different paths up a mountain. Along the path the views may differ, but from the mountaintop, the ultimate experience is the same.

Some techniques of meditation use mantras (as is discussed in this book) while other traditions use different practices, often focusing on awareness of breath. Whatever practice you use, it is important that you do it regularly and conscientiously. Different techniques are appropriate for different students, who may have varying personalities, inclinations, and capacities. Learn one method, apply it consistently and regularly over time, and observe what responses you seem to be making to the practice.

The practice of meditation using Breath Awareness alone is not sufficient, because the aspirant should learn to go beyond even the conscious and unconscious mind. Some traditions lead students to go beyond the conscious and unconscious mind, while other methods are limited to Breath Awareness alone. It is essential to learn to develop a comfortable, still posture, and then to become aware of the breath, but a human being is a thinking being, too, and he or she cannot ignore dealing with the various levels of the mind. Therefore, a method that leads the aspirant to go beyond all the levels of mind is a higher method of meditation. We do not condemn any method of meditation, but some are complete and some are incomplete. Eventually, the aspirant has to become aware of his or her essential nature, the source of consciousness, from which consciousness flows on various degrees and grades. The center of consciousness lies beyond body, senses, breath, and mind; therefore a method that is comprehensive and leads to the removal of all barriers is the best method.

Q: Should I use an alarm clock to time my meditation?

A: From the very beginning one should learn to strengthen his or her *sankalpa shakti* (or power of will and resolve) by resolving to oneself that he or she will rise on time and meditate for 10, 15, or 20 minutes. The mind is the greatest of all timekeepers, and as you progress, you will find that the mind wakes you up for your meditation. Nothing external is really needed when you have decided that you want to wake and meditate at a particular time.

Generally, it's not necessary to use an alarm clock to time the meditation itself, since in meditation, unlike the state of sleep, you will not lose consciousness or awareness of the passage of time. It's also rather unpleasant to end a tranquil meditation with the jarring tone of an alarm clock. If you're concerned about the time, keep a clock within view so you can check the time, or, better still, try to set up your meditation so that you don't feel so much time pressure—meditate earlier in the morning or in the evening when there are no duties or responsibilities awaiting you.

Q: What do I do if my legs begin to hurt or my feet fall asleep?

A: This often happens when the aspirant does not do enough physical exercise, but if you do begin to do stretching exercises before and after meditation, in a few days, you will not experience any physical discomfort, numbness or pain. If you experience discomfort or if your feet fall asleep, stretch out your legs and shift position for a few minutes. You can massage or stretch out the muscles and then, when your legs feel comfortable, resume your position. You will find that the length of time that you can sit comfortably will gradually increase as you form a habit, and in a few months the body will not feel the way it did in the beginning. Most modern people don't spend much time sitting on the floor, so initially, some postures will be less comfortable; however, you will probably find that as you become accustomed to your position, it feels increasingly natural. While it is commonplace for the body to have some initial adjustment to sitting (or any other new exercise) remember that you should never push your body to the point of pain. Exercise before and after the practice of meditation is important in helping to maintain good blood circulation.

Q: Sometimes my meditation is good and sometimes it is full of disturbances. How can I deal with this situation?

A: When the mind remains preoccupied by worldly wants and desires, these will interfere with the aspirant's experience during meditation. In such a case, one should develop a firm determination and learn to let go of all the thoughts that are coming forward in the mind and asking the aspirant for their fulfillment. Therefore, before one sits in meditation, it is important to have a determined mind and to inspire oneself by doing Breath Awareness. Decide not to be disturbed no matter what type of thoughts come into the conscious mind from the storehouse of merits and demerits, the unconscious mind. When students learn to witness their thinking process without becoming involved with the images, feelings, thoughts, and interests, then no thoughts—good and bad, helpful and unhelpful—can disturb them.

Q: Sometimes the body itches, the head tilts to one side or the other, or other symptoms such as yawning occur. What is the correct way of dealing with these disturbances?

A: Such disturbances occur during the preliminary stages of meditation. If one does not overeat, learns to keep the mind free from preoccupations, and observes the body, such dis-turbances can be checked easily.

Q: Why do I seem to become fearful in meditation?

A: This problem often occurs in those who have avoided knowing and becoming aware of their subtle thoughts, desires, suppressions, and repressions, as well as those who want to escape from self awareness, not wanting to analyze or understand their thinking processes.

Actually, a student is always safe during his or her meditation periods, because the closer that one is to the Reality and awareness, the safer one becomes. It is true that in meditation, hidden motivations, suppressions, and repressions do appear and become conscious, but the aspirant should increase his or her inner strength and allow these factors to come to awareness and then learn to let go of such thoughts so they do not continue to distract the mind. Sincere effort and practicing one's meditation consistently, at a regular time will, with firm determination, help the student to eventually overcome such hurdles and obstacles that arise in one's own mind.

Q: What is japa? How does it help to deepen meditation?

A: Japa is a mental repetition of the mantra and it is a very helpful tool for keeping the mind focused on maintaining the awareness of the center of consciousness. One can do japa all the time, in all situations and conditions. The silent technique of practicing japa without moving the tongue is one of the best ways of doing japa. The mind has a habit of always thinking of and obsessing about both the desirable and undesirable objects or events of the world. Keeping the mind busy doing japa is an accomplishment, and when japa becomes *ajapa* japa, (effortless and spontaneous), this process creates inner comfort, joy, peace, and happiness. If japa is done with feeling and not mere routine repetition, then it helps the student in attaining *mahabhava* (ecstasy). In all spiritual traditions of the world, some form of japa is recommended. It is one of the great supports and aids for an aspirant of meditation. Japa can be done using a *mala* or set of beads, or it can be done only mentally. If you use a mala, you move the bead each time you repeat the mantra.

Q: How do I know when I need a teacher and how do I find one?

A: When the aspirant begins to examine the

momentary and transitory nature of the objects of the external world, then he or she is no longer fully satisfied with them, and tries to understand his or her own internal states, questioning the purpose of life. Often, such a student studies the sayings of the sages. It is during this period of searching and seeking that students find that they need a guide. There is an ancient saying, which is true, that when a student has a burning desire to know, is sincerely seeking, and is prepared, then the teacher appears.

All aspirants and seekers should know that a teacher is always selfless and knows the state of mind of the aspirant and guides him or her accordingly. Do not search for a teacher, but prepare yourself first, and you will find a teacher. Those teachers who are selfish and dominating, or who selfishly use the resources of aspirants, can never really guide aspirants. Teachers who are selfless, experienced, and who practice meditation, know whether aspirants are actually prepared to tread the path. It is true that a competent teacher is a grace from God.

I advise seekers not to run here and there in search of teachers but rather, to prepare themselves by watching their own mind, action, and speech, for there is a teacher within everyone, and that is her or his own conscience. If we ignore that teacher, then the teacher outside will be of no use to us. Learning to listen to the conscience is a great preparation on the path of spirituality. Sometimes the ego comes forward and misguides us. The mind is a magician who can play many tricks, but the aspirant will learn to recognize when the "guidance" is not his or her conscience but due to an ego problem. I advise students to pray to the mighty Self within, for those prayers are always heard. A true prayer is always answered.

Q: How does one know that he or she is progressing?

A: Progressing on the path of spirituality is not like progressing in the external world. Progressing means developing a peaceful and joyous mind. Then, the student does not feel agitated or excited. This inner experience is a sufficient indication of the progress of the aspirant. The aspirant is bound to meet someone on the path of spirituality who shares similar goals, for the law of nature is, similar attracts similar.

Q: How do I know which path is best for me?

A: It is true that aspirants cannot tread a path if they are not prepared to do so. There are many diverse paths, but the goal is only one. The path in which you find inner satisfaction is your own path. Become aware of what path you feel is right for you.

Q: Can meditation cure emotional problems?

A: Meditation is the highest of all therapies, provided it is systematically practiced. Gradually, one learns to deal with one's own problems, fears, and habit patterns. Every human being has the capacity to advance and is fully equipped to deal even with gigantic problems, provided one follows his or her path with firm determination and sincerity. When your human efforts are completed, and if you still do not find peace within, then, in such cases, surrender yourself to the Self of all, the Lord of Life. Such self-surrender is the highest of all methods.

Q: Are there any dangers in practicing meditation?

A: Meditation is not at all dangerous, but if one is not prepared, then sitting and closing one's eyes and hallucinating is a sheer waste of time and energy. One should understand the whole method and gradually train oneself to be an "insider," for a human being is taught to learn, watch, verify and know things only in the external world. Learning to look, find, and see within is an entirely different path. Therefore, learning to practice meditation systematically is useful.

Many teachers claim that their methods are a "shortcut," and that other methods are lengthy. Some teachers who have a desire for publicity and self-gratification boast about such nonsense. There is no such thing as a shortcut or a lengthy process; the path depends entirely on the student's capacity, sincerity, and determination. Do not be swayed by such propaganda, publicity or promotions. Work with yourself.

Q: What are the methods of deepening meditation?

A: The method of meditation makes the mind one-pointed and inward. When one has learned to arrange his or her worldly duties so that they don't create any obstacles and when one practices meditation punctually and regularly, then he or she finds it rewarding in a special way: the mind becomes penetrative, one-pointed, and starts to fathom the subtler levels of life. These symptoms are the symptoms of the deepening of meditation.

Q: How does one develop a "feeling" for the mantra?

A: In the beginning, remembering the mantra technically is what is needed. Later on, the aspirant starts to experience joy because this habit becomes a part of his or her life. You actually love your habits, and when the japa becomes an irreplaceable habit of life, then you feel delighted by the mantra.

Q: What is the final outcome of meditation? What can we expect?

A: The books all say that the final outcome is the attainment of *samadhi.* There are various types of samadhi, but I can tell you that a meditator can attain the highest state of wisdom, in which the mind cannot and does not pose any questions, because all questions are answered and all problems are resolved. This delightful state of mind brings tranquility in the external world and permanent peace within. The meditator remains aware of Truth at every moment and becomes fearless, for he or she remembers the Lord of Life in every breath, and lives in the world unaffected by worldly turmoil.

Q: What is the difference between meditation and mental japa?

A: Japa "leads" the meditator and is a constant companion, which helps him or her to cross all the intervening barriers and obstacles, but finally japa leads one to silence. Silence is the greatest of all attainments. It is an experience in which one remains fully conscious and aware of the Reality or Self, which is the Self of all and the universal Truth.

Q: Do diet and sexual activity affect one's meditation?

A: Of course these factors affect meditation, so the mind should not be encouraged to roam and obsess in sexual grooves all the time. Sex is a biological and emotional necessity to a certain age, although this appetite should be regulated. This should not become the prominent and dominating point of one's life.

As far as food is concerned, simple, fresh, nutritious food that is not overcooked is the best for helping the student of meditation. However, even though foods that are rich in nutrients are most healthy, overeating is neither healthy nor conducive to meditation. Meditation should not be done either when one is hungry or just after one has eaten.

Q: How long will it take for a sincere student to attain the final goal?

A: This depends on the quality of one's internal states and determination, as well as the punctuality and regularity that he or she maintains in meditation practice. Some students become excited and emotional about wanting to attain the highest state. They practice enthusiastically for a few days, but then their interest changes and wanes, and they stop practicing. However, those who continue to practice their meditation with regularity and determination surely attain the highest wisdom in a short time. An aspirant has many fantasies, and through meditation these fantasies are replaced by fancies, desires or experiences, or expectations of miracles, but when a student understands that these experiences are not helpful, then he or she discourages them and goes beyond the mire of delusion, treading the path of light.

Recommendations
for Further Study

The following will be especially helpful in advancing your understanding and practice of meditation:

The Art of Joyful Living	Swami Rama
Creative Use of Emotion	Swami Rama
Lectures on Yoga	Swami Rama
Living with the Himalayan Masters	Swami Rama
Path of Fire and Light Vols I, II	Swami Rama
Hatha Yoga Manual I	Samskrti and Veda
Hatha Yoga Manual II	Samskrti and Judith Franks
Transition to Vegetarianism	
	Rudolph M. Ballentine, M.D.

You may also find several relaxation and meditation tapes to be useful, including:

31 and 61 Points
Guided Meditation for Beginners
A Guide to Intermediate Meditation
First Step Toward Advanced Meditation

All books and takes are available from Himalayan Publishers. Call toll-free 1-800-822-4547 for a catalog or further information.

Appendix A:
Relaxation Exercises

Tension/Relaxation Exercise

This exercise is done for 3 minutes at the beginning of your hatha yoga session. It can be practiced for several weeks or until the body and mind have started letting go of tension through the practice of hatha yoga postures, breathing exercises, and meditation.

TECHNIQUE

Lie in the corpse posture, relaxed and breathing evenly.

Tense all the muscles of the face, pulling them toward the tip of the nose. Then release the tension and relax.

Gently close the eyes, and keep them closed throughout the rest of the exercise.

Gently roll the head from side to side several times.

Pull the shoulders forward. Gently release and relax.

Tense the right arm in a subtle manner without making a fist or lifting the arm off the floor. Do not focus exclusively on tensing just the external muscles; take your mind to deeper within the muscle structure. Then release the tension and relax.

Repeat with the left arm.

Tense the hips and the buttocks. Then release the tension and relax.

Tense the right leg in the same manner that you tensed the right arm. Then release the tension and relax.

Repeat with the left leg.

Starting at the toes, relax the body from the toes, through the legs, torso, arms, neck, and head.[1]

Complete Relaxation Exercise

Before meditating it is beneficial to do a concentrated relaxation exercise. There are many such exercises. The one described here relaxes the skeletal muscles, eliminates any fatigue or strain following the postures, and energizes both the mind and the body. During this exercise keep the mind alert and concentrated on your breath as you progressively relax your muscles. In the beginning you should practice this exercise for only ten minutes, because beyond that time the mind usually begins to wander and you may find yourself drifting toward sleep.

1. Reprinted from *Hatha Yoga Manual II.*

TECHNIQUE

Lie in the corpse posture with the eyes gently closed. Inhale and exhale through the nostrils slowly, smoothly, and deeply. There should be no noise, jerks, or pauses in the breath; let the inhalations and exhalations flow naturally without exertion in one continuous movement. Keep the body still.

Mentally travel through the body and relax the top of the head, forehead, eyebrows, space between the eyebrows, eyes, eyelids, cheeks, and nose. Then exhale and inhale completely four times, breathing diaphragmatically.

Exhaling, relax the mouth, jaw, chin, neck, shoulders, upper arms, lower arms, wrists, hands, fingers, and fingertips. Feel as if you are inhaling from the fingertips, up the arms, shoulders, and face to the nostrils, and then exhaling back to the fingertips. Then exhale and inhale completely four times.

Relax the fingertips, fingers, hands, wrists, lower arms, upper arms, shoulders, upper back, and chest. Concentrate at the center of the chest, and exhale and inhale completely four times.

Relax the stomach, abdomen, lower back, hips, thighs, knees, calves, ankles, feet, and toes.

Exhale as though your whole body is exhaling, and inhale as though your whole body is inhaling. Expel all your tension, worries, and anxieties; inhale vital energy, peace, and relaxation. Exhale and inhale completely four times.

Relax the toes, feet, ankles, calves, thighs, knees, hips,

lower back, abdomen, stomach and chest. Concentrating at the center of the chest, exhale and inhale completely four times.

Relax the upper back, shoulders, upper arms, lower arms, wrists, hands, fingers, and fingertips. Then exhale and inhale completely four times.

Relax the fingertips, fingers, hands, wrists, lower arms, upper arms, shoulders, neck, chin, jaw, mouth, and nostrils. Then exhale and inhale completely four times.

Relax the cheeks, eyelids, eyes, eyebrows, space between the eyebrows, forehead, and top of the head. Now, for 30 to 60 seconds, let your mind be aware of the calm and serene flow of the breath; let your mind make a gentle, conscious effort to guide your breath so that it remains smooth, calm, and deep, without any noise or jerks.

Slowly and gently open your eyes. Stretch the body. Try to maintain this calm, peaceful feeling throughout the day.

A taped relaxation exercise is available from the Himalayan Institute.

Appendix B:
Breathing Exercises

There are many pranayama (breathing) exercises. The following exercises are the most important for beginners.

The Complete Breath

The complete breath helps expand the capacity of the lungs and is excellent as a physical and mental energizing exercise. If possible, practice the exercise in front of an open window or out of doors.

When doing the exercise it may be helpful to imagine yourself as a glass of water being emptied and filled. When the water is poured out, the glass empties from the top to the bottom. When the water is poured in, the glass fills from the bottom to the top.

TECHNIQUE

Assume the simple standing posture.

Inhaling, fill the lower lungs, then the middle lungs, and then the upper lungs; simultaneously, raise the arms until they are overhead, palms touching, in a prayer position.

Exhaling, empty the upper lungs, then the middle lungs, and then the lower lungs as the arms are lowered back to the side.

Repeat the exercise 2 to 5 more times.

Diaphragmatic Breathing

Although breathing is one of our most vital functions, it is little understood and often done improperly. Most people breathe shallowly and haphazardly, going against the natural rhythmic movement of the body's respiratory system. Diaphragmatic breathing, on the other hand, promotes a natural, even breath movement that strengthens the nervous system and relaxes the body. The importance of deep, even breathing in meditation cannot be overemphasized.

Respiration is normally of either of two types or a combination of both: chest or abdominal. Chest breathing or shallow breathing is characterized by an outward movement of the upper chest. Deep abdominal breathing is characterized by an outward movement of the abdominal wall due to the contraction and descent of the diaphragm. Practitioners of yoga recognize a third type of breathing, known as diaphragmatic breathing, which focuses attention on the diaphragm in the lower rib cage. It is this method of breathing that is practiced during the asanas. Diaphragmatic breathing should not be confused with abdominal or belly breathing, which is also sometimes referred to as deep diaphragmatic breathing.

The principal muscle of diaphragmatic breathing, the diaphragm, is a strong, horizontal, dome-shaped muscle. It divides the thoracic cavity, which contains the heart and lungs, from the abdominal cavity, which contains the organs of digestion, reproduction, and excretion (see diagram, p. 118). The diaphragm is located approximately at mid-chest, in its relaxed or dome-shaped state.

During inhalation, the diaphragm contracts and flattens; it pushes downward, causing the upper abdominal muscles to relax and extend slightly and the lower "floating" ribs to flare slightly outward. In this position the lungs expand, creating a partial vacuum, which draws air into the chest cavity. During exhalation, the diaphragm relaxes and returns to its dome-shaped position. During this upward movement, the upper abdominal muscles contract, and carbon dioxide is forced from the lungs.

Diaphragmatic breathing has three important effects on the body:

1. In diaphragmatic breathing, unlike shallow breathing, the lungs fill completely, providing the body with sufficient oxygen.

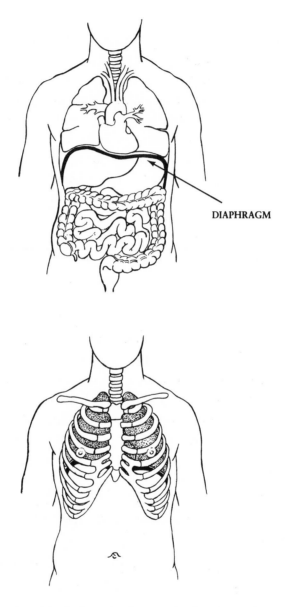

Location of the diaphragm in relation to the ribs and internal organs.

2. Diaphragmatic breathing forces the waste product of the respiratory process, carbon dioxide, from the lungs. When breathing shallowly, some carbon dioxide may remain trapped in the lungs, causing fatigue and nervousness.

3. The up and down motion of the diaphragm gently massages the abdominal organs; this increases circulation to these organs and thus aids in their functioning.

In diaphragmatic breathing a minimum amount of effort is used to receive a maximum amount of air; thus, it is our most efficient method of breathing.

TECHNIQUE

Lie on the back with the feet a comfortable distance apart. Gently close the eyes and place one hand on the upper abdomen and the other on the chest.

Inhale and exhale through the nostrils slowly, smoothly, and evenly, with no noise, jerks, or pauses in the breath. While inhaling, be aware of the upper abdominal muscles expanding and the lower ribs flaring out slightly. There should be little or no movement of the chest.

Practice this method of deep breathing 3 to 5 minutes daily until you clearly understand the movement of the diaphragm and the upper abdominal muscles. The body is designed to breathe diaphragmatically; gradually it should again become a natural function.

Nadi Shodhana

There are many methods of pranayama, each for a specific purpose. Nadi shodhana is a simple pranayama exercise that purifies the nadis, the subtle energy channels. It balances the flow of breath in the nostrils and the flow of energy in the nadis. Nadi shodhana should be practiced at least twice a day, in the morning and evening.

TECHNIQUE

1. Sit in the easy posture with the head, neck, and trunk straight. Inhalation and exhalation should be of equal duration. Do not force the breath; keep it slow, controlled, and free from sounds and jerks. With practice, gradually lengthen the duration of the inhalation and the exhalation.

2. Bring the right hand to the nose, folding the index finger and the middle finger so that the right thumb can be used to close the right nostril and the ring finger can be used to close the left nostril.

3. Close the passive nostril and exhale completely through the active nostril.

4. At the end of the exhalation, close the active nostril and inhale through the passive nostril slowly and completely. Inhalation and exhalation should be of equal duration.

5. Repeat this cycle of exhalation with the active nostril and inhalation with the passive nostril two more times.

6. At the end of the third inhalation with the passive nostril, exhale completely through the same nostril, keeping the active nostril closed with the finger or thumb.

7. At the end of the exhalation, close the passive nostril and inhale through the active nostril.

8. Repeat two more times the cycle of exhalation through the passive nostril and inhalation through the active nostril.

To summarize:

1	Exhale	Active
2	Inhale	Passive
3	Exhale	Active
4	Inhale	Passive
5	Exhale	Active
6	Inhale	Passive
7	Exhale	Passive
8	Inhale	Active
9	Exhale	Passive
10	Inhale	Active
11	Exhale	Passive
12	Inhale	Active

Place the hands on the knees and exhale and inhale through both nostrils evenly for three breath cycles. This completes one cycle of nadi shodhana.

Glossary

Ahamkara: Loosely translated as ego; together, manas, buddhi, chitta, and ahamkara comprise the functions of the mind. It is through this inner faculty that one identifies oneself with the objects of the world, such as "I am this body." It refers to a function of mind through which pure consciousness falsely identifies itself with non-self, material objects.

Ajapa japa: The spontaneous constant awareness of one's mantra; constant awareness of one's mantra with every breath of life.

Asana: A posture or pose; the meditative posture, carefully selected according to the nature and capacity of the student. A good student selects a sitting posture and learns to become accomplished in it.

Atman: Pure Consciousness, the true Self, the unchanging, eternal Truth that is beyond the entire manifest world.

AUM (or OM): Sound that represents the Absolute. According to the Upanishads, the word *AUM* consists of three letters—A, U, and M—representing waking, dreaming, and deep sleep. After the word *AUM*, there comes a state of silence that represents Absolute or transcendent Reality.

Bandhas: "Locks." Bodily gestures which establish connections between energy channels *(nadis)* and aid in controlling the flow of vital energy *(prana)* in the practice of *pranayama.*

Bhava: Emotion, mood, devotional state of mind, feeling.

Buddhi: The powerful faculty of intellect. Buddhi is the faculty of mind that has three main functions: It knows, decides, and judges.

Chitta: The pool of unconscious mind, into which all the impressions gathered by the senses are deposited, and from the bottom of which they arise to create a constant stream of random thoughts and associations.

Dhyana: Meditation; one-pointed state of mind that is not disturbed by any thought constructs.

Hatha Yoga: The science of physical health which developed out of the third limb of raja yoga, *asana.* It attempts, through postures and cleansing exercises, to prepare the student for higher practices in yoga.

Ida: One of the three principal energy channels flowing in the spinal cord. It controls the breath in the left nostril.

Japa: Repetition of one's mantra; constant japa is a great technique of making the mind one-pointed. Japa as a practice is complete in itself provided it is done with knowledge and with full devotion.

Kundalini: The inner fire or fundamental life-energy, the dormant fire, coiled energy. Kundalini in its dormant state resides at the base of the spine. By following a systematic discipline of pranayama, meditation, and mantra japa, one prepares oneself for kundalini awakening.

Kriya: Action, activity, as kriya yoga—a path of action.

Mahabhava: The state of ecstasy.

Maitri Asana: Friendship pose, a meditative posture sitting in a chair or on a platform.

Manas: Mind. One of the inner instruments that receives information from the external world with the help of the senses and presents it to the higher faculty of intellect. This particular faculty is also characterized by doubt.

Mantra: A combination of syllables, or words, corresponding to a particular energy vibration. The student, when initiated by a qualified teacher, utilizes the *mantra* as his object for meditation, and as he practices over a period of time it gradually leads his meditation deeper and deeper. Through constant practice of *japa* (repetition) within meditation and in active life, the power of the *mantra* and its essential teaching will gradually unfold (as its latent mental and spiritual energies are released).

Mudra: Certain bodily gestures, like the "finger lock," that are used to deepen meditation.

Nadi: Energy channel; one of the subtle channels of the body.

Nadi Shodhana: Literally, "purifying the *nadis.*" A breathing exercise that purifies the *nadis* in preparation for the higher practice of *pranayama.* Also known as "channel purification," or "alternate nostril breathing," it attempts to quiet the mind and regulate the breath by establishing a slow, even rhythm, without a pause between inhalation and exhalation.

Om: The highest of *mantras.* Its three letters, *A, U* and *M,* represent the elements of all trinities. There is also a silent fourth syllable symbolizing the transcendent "fourth" state of consciousness, which is pure spirit, or *samadhi.* A symbol of the highest realization and knowledge.

Padmasana: The lotus posture. A sitting posture for breathing exercises.

Patanjali: A sage who was the codifier of Yoga Science.

Pingala: The *nadi,* or energy channel, which is one of the three running parallel to the spinal column. It controls the flow of breath in the right nostril, and when this channel becomes active one's behavior is characterized by rationality, activity and energy.

Prana: The life force. In the yogic tradition, the life force prana is said to be tenfold, depending on its nature and function.

Pranayama: Expansion of, or voluntary control over the pranic force. Breath control; breathing exercise; the fourth rung of raja yoga. The science of gradually lengthening and controlling the physical breath in order to gain control over the movement of prana through the subtle body in higher stages of the practice.

Raja yoga: Royal path; the eightfold path of yoga as described by Patanjali in the *Yoga Sutras*.

Sadhana: Practice, spiritual endeavor. Literally, "accomplishing," or "fulfilling." Sadhana is the word for a student's sincere efforts along a particular path of practice toward Self-realization.

Samadhi: Spiritual absorption; the eighth rung of raja yoga. The tranquil state of mind in which fluctuations of the mind no longer arise.

Samskaras: Subtle impressions of past actions.

Sankalpa shakti: The power of dynamic will or resolution.

Shanti: Peace.

Shavasana: The Corpse posture. A posture for relaxation.

Siddhi: Accomplishment, perfection, achievement. In practicing yoga, as one progresses toward the center of consciousness, several advanced potentials unfold, which can be very attractive and distracting. The goal of yoga is not to become caught by the siddhis, but to go beyond.

Siddhasana: The Accomplished posture. A sitting posture used for breathing exercises and meditation.

Sukhasana: The Easy posture. A sitting posture used for breathing exercises and meditation.

Sushumna: The central energy channel or nadi that runs along the spinal column from the base to the crown of the head. The goal of preliminary breathing exercises is to open this central channel so that both nostrils are flowing equally, and then the mind enters a joyful state in which it easily attains a deep state of meditation.

Swarodaya: The ancient Science of Breath, by which the sages learned much about human functioning and the subtler energies.

Swastikasana: The Auspicious posture. A sitting posture used for breathing exercises and meditation.

Tattva: Element. There are five elements: earth, water, fire, air, and space.

Trataka: The practice of gazing in order to strengthen concentration.

Yoga: The word *yoga* is generated from the Sanskrit root *yuj* which means *union,* as well as the systematic *application* of certain practices with tested and proven effects and benefits.

Yoga Sutras: A manual on raja yoga, compiled by the sage, Patanjali, circa 200 B.C. It forms the basic outline from which all systems of yoga philosophy and practice claim their origin.

About the Author

Yogi, scientist, philosopher, humanitarian, and mystic poet, Swami Rama is the founder and spiritual head of the Himalayan International Institute of Yoga Science and Philosophy, with its headquarters in Honesdale, Pennsylvania, and therapy and educational centers throughout the world. He was born in a Himalayan valley of Uttar Pradesh, India, in 1925 and was initiated and anointed in early childhood by a great sage of the Himalayas. He studied with many adepts, and then traveled to Tibet to study with his grandmaster. From 1949 to 1952 he held the prestige and dignity of Shankaracharya (spiritual leader) in Karvirpitham in the South of India. He then returned to the Himalayas to intensify his meditative practices in the cave monasteries and to establish an ashram in Rishikesh.

Later he continued his investigation of Western psychology and philosophy at several European universities, and he taught in Japan before coming to the United States in 1969. The following year he served as a consultant to the Voluntary Controls Project of the Research Department of the Menninger Foundation. There he demonstrated, under laboratory conditions, precise control over his autonomic nervous system and brain. The findings of that research increased the scientific community's understanding of the human ability to control autonomic functioning and to attain previously unrecognized levels of consciousness.

Shortly thereafter, Swami Rama founded the Himalayan Institute as a means to synthesize the ancient teachings of the East with the modern approaches of the West. He has played a major role in bringing the insights of yoga psychology and philosophy to the attention of the physicians and psychologists of the West. He continues to teach students around the world while intensifying his writing and meditative practices. He is the author of many books and currently spends most of his time in the mountains of Northern India and in Pennsylvania, U.S.A.

The main building of the national headquarters, Honesdale, Pa.

The Himalayan Institute

Since its establishment in 1971, the Himalayan Institute has been dedicated to helping individuals develop themselves physically, mentally, and spiritually, as well as contributing to the transformation of society. All the Institute programs—educational, therapeutic, research—emphasize holistic health, yoga, and meditation as tools to help achieve those goals. Institute programs combine the best of ancient wisdom and modern science, of Eastern teachings and Western technologies. We invite you to join with us in this ongoing process of personal growth and development.

Our beautiful national headquarters, on a wooded 400-acre campus in the Pocono Mountains of northeastern Pennsylvania, provides a peaceful, healthy setting for our seminars, classes, and training programs in the principles and practices of holistic living. Students from around the world have joined us here for the past fifteen years to attend programs in such diverse areas as biofeedback and stress reduction, hatha yoga, meditation, diet and nutrition, philosophy and metaphysics, and practical psychology for better living. We see the realization of our human potentials as a lifelong quest, leading to increased health, creativity, and happiness, awareness and improving the quality of their life.

The Institute is a nonprofit organization. Your membership in the Institute helps to support its programs. Please call or write for information on becoming a member.

Institute Programs, Services, and Facilities

All Institute programs share an emphasis on conscious, holistic living and personal self-development. You may enjoy any of a number of diverse programs, including:

- Special weekend or extended seminars to teach skills and techniques for increasing your ability to be healthy and enjoy life

- Holistic health services

- Professional training for health professionals

- Meditation retreats and advanced meditation instruction

- Cooking and nutritional training
- Hatha yoga and exercise workshops
- Residential programs for self-development

The Himalayan Institute Charitable Hospital

A major aspect of the Institute's work around the world is its construction and management of a modern, comprehensive hospital and holistic health facility in the mountain area of Dehra Dun, India. Outpatient facilities are already providing medical care to those in need, and also mobile units have been equipped to visit outlying villages. Construction work on the main hospital building is progressing as scheduled.

We welcome financial support to help with construction and the provision of services. We also welcome donations of medical supplies, equipment, or professional expertise. If you would like further information on the Hospital, please contact us.

Himalayan Institute Publications

Art of Joyful Living	Swami Rama
Book of Wisdom (Ishopanishad)	Swami Rama
A Call to Humanity	Swami Rama
Celestial Song/Gobind Geet	Swami Rama
Choosing a Path	Swami Rama
The Cosmic Drama: Bichitra Natak	Swami Rama
Enlightenment Without God	Swami Rama
Exercise Without Movement	Swami Rama
Freedom from the Bondage of Karma	Swami Rama
Indian Music, Volume I	Swami Rama
Inspired Thoughts of Swami Rama	Swami Rama
Japji: Meditation in Sikhism	Swami Rama
Lectures on Yoga	Swami Rama
Life Here and Hereafter	Swami Rama
Living with the Himalayan Masters	Swami Rama
Love Whispers	Swami Rama
Marriage, Parenthood, and Enlightenment	Swami Rama
Meditation and Its Practice	Swami Rama
Path of Fire and Light, Vol. I	Swami Rama
Path of Fire and Light, Vol. II	Swami Rama
Perennial Psychology of the Bhagavad Gita	Swami Rama
A Practical Guide to Holistic Health	Swami Rama
Sukhamani Sahib: Fountain of Eternal Joy	Swami Rama
The Wisdom of the Ancient Sages	Swami Rama
Creative Use of Emotion	Swami Rama, Swami Ajaya
Science of Breath	Swami Rama, Rudolph Ballentine, M.D., Alan Hymes, M.D.
Yoga and Psychotherapy	Swami Rama, Rudolph Ballentine, M.D., Swami Ajaya, Ph.D.

Himalayan Mountain Cookery	Martha Ballentine
The Yoga Way Cookbook	Himalayan Institute
Meditation in Christianity	Himalayan Institute
Art and Science of Meditation	Himalayan Institute
Inner Paths	Himalayan Institute
Chants from Eternity	Himalayan Institute
Spiritual Diary	Himalayan Institute
Blank Books	Himalayan Institute

To order or to request a free mail order catalog call or write

The Himalayan Publishers
RR 1, Box 400
Honesdale, PA 18431
Toll-Free 1-800-822-4547